WHY
JACOB
MATTERS

Change Culture and Cultivate
Talent by Listening, Leading, and
Building Accountability

JOHN HIESTER

ISBN: 978-1-4834-9275-9 (sc)
ISBN: 978-1-4834-9276-6 (hc)
ISBN: 978-1-4834-9249-0 (e)

Library of Congress Control Number: 2019910908

Cover photo taken by Logan Allen

Lulu Publishing Services rev. date: 08/14/2019

*To my daughters, Amanda and Ashley, for teaching
me so many lessons about leadership.*

ABOUT THE AUTHOR

John Hiester took his first management position in 1989 and opened his first business in 2002. Since then, Hiester Automotive Group has added four locations, growing by more than 300 percent in seventeen years, from a dozen employees to more than 300. Hiester has served on many boards, including the First Bank Advisory Board and the Cary Christian School Board. At the time of this publication, he serves as the North Carolina Automobile Dealers Association's Board  Vice-Chairman. He was President of the Angier Chamber of Commerce and Angier Man of the Year in 2008. He has been married to his wife, Lisa, since 1985 and has two daughters, Amanda and Ashley. He frequently speaks and teaches about business process, leadership, and communication. *Inspiration* is his favorite word.

INTRODUCTION

Why Jacob Matters

Organizations don't just rely on their people, they are their people.

I believed in this bedrock principle before I started my own company, nearly twenty years ago. I certainly believed in it while working in my first management position back in 1989, and probably long before that.

Within days of getting my first real job, in fact, I understood that finding, engaging, and retaining quality team members is *the* key to success in business. That part was easy. Figuring out the best ways to turn this belief into reality took me another thirty years – and is very much a continuing quest.

Not a week passes that I don't work on some new business strategy, refine an approach, or sharpen a trusted tool. I am a business-process geek of the first order, passionate about finding better ways to manage and motivate people. Show me a business problem, and I will obsess over the process or program that can address it until I'm convinced I have the best solution.

A few years ago I confronted just such a problem, one that anyone in business can relate to – how to attract and retain the college-educated career-minded millennials who were vital to the future of our organization. In response to this challenge, my senior leadership team and I developed a program that we thought would be an excellent way to do two things. First, it was a powerful tool for recruiting, training, and engaging employees like Jacob, a sharp worker not long out of college, the kind of guy we hoped would stick around and build a career with us. Second, it would change our business model to more accurately reflect the way consumers shop in the digital age.

We felt that this program was vital to our future, integral to a change in culture that had been years in the making. A few months after it rolled out, however, Jacob was quitting and I was left wondering what had gone wrong.

Talking to Jacob about the problems with our new program and processes as he saw them was an eye-opener for me. During the following months, we worked to address the issues he laid out and to make sure that our efforts to create a new organizational culture and to engage employees like Jacob would succeed.

This is very much a practical book about business strategy and process. It includes concrete lessons readers can begin applying tomorrow on effective communication, core values, smart metrics, world-class training, culture change, and more.

It is also, however, a human story about the founder of a company and a new employee and the ways that they learned from each other. It's the tale of an experienced boss who becomes a humble student and an inexperienced worker who falls into the role of teacher.

I go through books on business and leadership like fish go through water. There's always one if not several of these volumes on my nightstand, and I learn something valuable from all of them. Despite their utility, though, many are fairly dry, some downright boring. As someone who loves a good story, my gut instinct is always to illustrate a point or lesson with narrative. That approach is more interesting to me as a reader, and it's what I've set out to do here as a writer.

The overarching narrative in these pages is the story of my interaction with Jacob, who is really a stand-in for all the college-educated career-minded team members we hope to recruit, develop, and engage. Each chapter also kicks off with a story of its own to demonstrate whatever lessons regarding leadership, communication, process, etc. I want to convey there. Some of those stories involve my business. Some involve family or other parts of my life, but all bear directly on the subject at hand. The greatest lessons I ever learned on leadership and communication, for example, came from a seven-year-old named Amanda, as I'll explain in Chapter 2.

On a practical note, each chapter ends with an exercise that walks readers through the concrete steps that will help them put the techniques we've explored into practice – everything from establishing core values to building career ladders to troubleshooting and course correction.

It is my hope that this strategy has produced a book that's not only helpful for leaders of all levels at organizations of all kinds, but also one that's compelling and fun to read. Many of my examples come from the automotive industry because it's what I know best, but the lessons apply equally well to any organization that needs to hire, develop, engage, and manage people – which is to say, all organizations. The local retail store, the software developer, the painting contractor, the young trade association with three employees, and the old business with 300 – all will benefit from these strategies.

This is definitely not a textbook, and it's not written primarily for CEOs, though chief executives might benefit from it. My target audience is those on their way up – supervisors, middle managers, senior leaders, small-business owners hoping to grow.

The idea of growth comes up repeatedly in this book because it's central to my story. I opened my first business in 2002. Since then, Hiester Automotive Group has added four locations, growing by more than 300 percent in seventeen years. We had a dozen employees at our first store and now have more than 300. Along the way, I took on bigger roles in my industry and community, too. I have served on many Boards, including the First Bank Advisory Board and the Cary Christian School Board, and I'm currently the North Carolina Automobile Dealers Association's Vice-Chairman. I was president of the Angier Chamber of Commerce and

Angier Man of the Year in 2008, and I've done all of this as our business continues to expand.

My obsession with business process, you see, was born partly of necessity. Designing effective, intelligent processes is really the only way to grow – or at least, the only way to do so without sending your blood pressure through the roof.

My underlying thesis here is incredibly simple. Great leaders decide what they want. They take the time to determine what *great* looks like, and then they devise a process to get there. The chapters that follow contain various tools and techniques to help you put this idea into effect and to drive home my central premise, the idea that I hope every reader takes away from this book:

You get what you settle for if you don't know what you want.

CHAPTER 1
Losing Jacob

Why did the millennial who seemed to be a perfect fit quit?

I woke up one Tuesday morning after a restless night in which two questions interrupted my sleep: why was my employee Jacob really quitting, and what was wrong with the new program we had hired him to be a part of?

I went into work tired that morning, took care of some business first thing, then headed over to our store in Lillington, North Carolina, the one where Jacob worked. After parking my car, I spotted him driving off the lot. I waved him over and he pulled to the side. I could have let him go, caught him when he returned or the next day, but these two questions were urgent. Shading my eyes, I crossed to his car and leaned in the window.

"I hear you're leaving us," I said.

"Yes, sir. I am," said Jacob, a little sheepish but looking me in the eye. I pride myself on being a straightforward person, and I'd been struck when hiring Jacob three months earlier by his similarly direct disposition and by the politeness still present today. During his first weeks with the company, his face seemed perpetually lit by a smile – affability his default setting – but about a month earlier, I noticed that it was gone.

"Why are you quitting?"

"Well, sir, my sister in Wilmington just had her second baby, and she needs help. I want to be there for her."

"I think there's more to it, Jacob. Why are you *really* leaving?"

"No, sir, that's it. My sister really does need help."

It was the answer I expected, the same one he'd given his manager a couple days earlier and then again yesterday when I asked his boss to probe deeper, to find out what was really going on. After questioning Jacob further, his manager had assured me that our new hire was simply quitting for family reasons.

I didn't buy it.

Jacob was in his early twenties, a sharp guy fresh from college with a positive, hopeful attitude – smart, kind, ambitious, a quick study. When we hired him, he had a spark in his eyes that I recognized. After three months, though, I noticed the light fading from Jacob's face. He no longer had that sparkle or the smile I'd grown accustomed to. His shoulders slouched, if ever so slightly. I suspected that he'd gone from *fired-up* about a job to *putting up* with one.

As soon as I'd noticed Jacob's engagement slipping, I asked the general manager of the store what was wrong. Nothing, he assured me, Jacob was doing just fine. A month later, Jacob was quitting. There was more to this story, and I needed to hear it.

We went back and forth for a few minutes, Jacob insisting that he was leaving to help his sister, and me probing for some deeper motivation. I did not doubt that his sister needed help, I explained, or that he wanted to provide it (his willingness to help his family was just more evidence of the solid character that made him a good hire in the first place), but I felt certain that something about his job was making this decision easier.

"Oh," he said, relenting, or perhaps finally taking my point. Jacob took a deep breath. "I told you why I'm leaving, but I guess what you're really asking is, why am I not staying?"

He started to explain, and I said, "Have you got a few minutes? Can we go sit down?"

Jacob followed me into the store, where we commandeered an office. He did not speak in bullet points during our impromptu meeting, but he might as well have, so succinct was his list of the eight big problems he had with his position, delivered off the cuff and straight from the heart. Here they are in summary:

- The company's leadership was not demonstrating its core values.
- Jacob's expectations / job description did not match the reality, i.e. the managers were not utilizing his position as intended.
- He felt undervalued. His position was not as important as management had said it would be.
- The initial training was great, then nothing.
- He did not see growth opportunity.
- He did not feel that we were providing ways for him to contribute to the community as outlined in our mission statement and core focus.
- Although the company culture initially felt welcoming, in the day-to-day business, it did not.
- There was no regular coaching; in fact, he often felt as if he / his position was in the way.

I am always disappointed to see a smart, hardworking employee leave but in this case, I was crushed. It is no exaggeration to say that I believed that the future of my business depended on Jacob, or a "Jacob" – this sort of employee filling this kind of position, a new role we'd worked hard to create. Jacob's leaving after just three months felt like a major failure – mine, not his – one made all the more painful because we'd devised strategies specifically to cultivate team members like Jacob.

He was the green employee, and I owned the company, but it was his turn to educate me.

Before I get to my response to the problems he detailed, I want to explain why Jacob's departure and the eight reasons that he gave for it hit me so hard. In order to tell you Jacob's whole story, I need to backtrack to explain how we created his position and identified him as an ideal candidate for it in the first place.

The story will be a familiar one to any reader who is part of an organization where growth and innovation depend on finding, motivating, and retaining college-educated career-minded millennials. Many readers face the same dilemma I faced that day in Lillington and can learn from both my mistakes and the techniques we used to correct course.

MEETING THE CHALLENGES OF GROWTH

Hiester Automotive Group opened its first dealership in Angier, North Carolina, in 2002. The company we started enjoyed early success and expanded steadily. Today, it has grown by more than 300 percent, and includes four locations. The business went from a dozen employees to almost 300 in sixteen years. This sort of expansion does not occur without growing pains and believe me, we experienced our share. One of the things I hope to do in this book is offer strategies for organizations that are growing, or trying to grow – techniques that both foster expansion and make it as smooth and healthy as possible.

I say "organization," by the way, because as I pointed out in the introduction, the strategies I'll present here apply as well to nonprofits, schools, churches, trade associations, political groups, etc. as they do to businesses. They apply to the mom-and-pop corner store with three employees and to the accounting firm with three floors of CPAs.

The most difficult piece of the puzzle as any organization grows is always its *people*. Leading a dozen people is relatively easy. Two dozen becomes more difficult, and by the time you get to thirty, it's tough to keep priorities from slipping. As an owner or manager, you cannot be everywhere or keep tabs on everything. How do you guarantee that the organization is hiring, training, and leading optimally, in the way that you intend? How do you ensure quality products, service, and experiences for those you serve when you're no longer on the front line?

I asked myself these questions repeatedly in the early 2000s as I added employees and my business grew. One of my early answers was to create a mission statement, which I did after four or five years in business. Here it is:

We will provide quality products and honest, unparalleled service to all who enter our doors. We strive to make a difference in all our associates' lives by training, educating, and motivating them to grow professionally in a team environment. At Hiester Automotive Group, it is our desire that the relationships we form with our customers last a lifetime. We will strive to be good stewards in the communities in which we operate through our support of local activities and civic groups. Hiester Automotive Group's goal as a successful business is to be honest and fair to our customers and associates and to always deliver a "World-Class Experience."

I will talk more about mission statements later, but as you can see from ours, the idea is to provide cohesion and a common sense of purpose, or mission – to spell out the *why* that gives the team its foundation. Creating a mission statement allowed my expanding team to state clearly that no matter what job you do within the organization, which location you work at, or how long you've been there, we *all* hold certain things dear – a commitment to honesty, unparalleled service, a world-class experience, and lifelong relationships. Those were promises I wanted all employees to make to our customers every day.

We also promised to support the community – something I deeply believed in but perhaps had never stated so explicitly – and I pledged to employees that our organization would be much more than simply a way to pay the mortgage. Training, education, and motivation were priorities not only because they resulted in better service for customers, but also because they provided avenues for employee growth and fulfillment. I had not yet developed most of the strategies I'm going to share with you in these pages, but even in those first years in business, I knew in my bones that employees who saw clear paths for their own growth at work would make the organization's growth that much smoother.

The mission statement was not just an idea for me or for the organization. We used it in hiring, training, and daily operations. It was displayed prominently, and the principles it set forth helped guide our growth. Yes, we were adding team members and new layers of management, but the mission statement kept us all on the same page – or so I thought.

One day, I realized that our employees' processes and protocols in certain areas varied widely, depending on the store and the employees. Some of their approaches were terrible and some were great, but even the best ones varied from mine and from each other. These team members had been trained at different places all over the country and their approaches were full of inconsistencies. We decided to start from scratch and developed a consistent training program, one that we now believe to be the best in the industry.

PRIORITIZING PROCESS OVER TALENT

As we developed consistent training and a mission statement, I came to believe that the best friend of any leader at any organization is *Written Repeatable Process.* Lots of my employees and managers had terrific training, but making our training consistent – standardized, clearly written out, part of a procedure – was a game changer.

I will return to this idea of Written Repeatable Process again and again in these pages because it is foundational for my organization, and is, I believe, the only way to manage growth, multiple locations, and an expanding team – or the only way to do it effectively while remaining sane. In addition to helping organizations manage growth, Written Repeatable Process spurs growth, too, by realizing efficiencies, instilling standards, guaranteeing consistency, and pointing the way to solid measurables.

Focusing on Written Repeatable Process was life-changing for me and for the organization. Previously, as is the case with so many businesses, we were a talent-driven organization. We hired the stars from other companies – the top sellers, the best accountants, the hotshot mechanics, the workers with the lengthy resumes. It was what you might call a lone-wolf model, and make no mistake, it brought us some very talented people who achieved impressive results.

Becoming more of a process-driven organization did not mean that we ignored talent, only that process now had primacy. Core values first, talent second, and the lone wolves who could not think about the good of the pack or the values the rest of us shared had to find the door, no matter how skilled they were.

What do I mean by *values*? These were the principles that made us who we were and great at what we did. We used considerable energy and a formal process to determine our core values. Defining them was not merely a pro-forma exercise or way to create wall hangings. In a process-driven environment, our core values (character / integrity, servant attitude, professional, get-it-done attitude, loves people) became the rudder guiding the ship. We used them to hire, train, measure, and motivate employees. Working in conjunction with our mission statement, they became fundamental to how we managed, made decisions, and formulated strategy.

Using core values to set our standards meant losing some top performers, but in every instance, removing the lone wolf brought the rest of the team up a notch and led to better overall results. The lone wolves, by the way, often left amicably, since plenty of organizations value talent over process and people generally want to live in a system where they'll thrive, surrounded by those with similar values.

What I'm describing here in miniature and will explore in depth throughout the book adds up to a deep change in organizational culture. Management is difficult, especially when an organization is growing, or hoping to, but it becomes exponentially easier when you focus on organizational culture.

Managing a company without managing its culture is like setting off on a journey without a map or trying to ride a horse without reins. Having a mission statement, solid consistent training, and Written Repeatable Processes in all possible areas establishes expectations, builds cohesion, and frees your employees because they know what is expected of them. It puts everyone on the same page. All of these elements rest on a foundation of shared core values that keep the entire organization focused on its purpose, or *why*, judging every decision against your most deeply held common beliefs.

Like most cultural shifts, ours did not occur in a vacuum. My business and our entire industry – and I can just about guarantee that this is true of yours, too – was being transformed by the Internet and the emerging digital landscape. Information about products and pricing was becoming widely available and easier to compare than ever before. The expectations of service were rising, and the art of negotiation – once the key component in my business – was dying. Many consumers did not want to purchase our products in the same ways they used to, and it was becoming increasingly difficult to differentiate ourselves from the competition.

In addition to helping us become process-oriented, our core values were at the center of our efforts to set ourselves apart and remain competitive in a rapidly changing landscape.

BUILDING A NEW MODEL

This culture change at my organization and our growing focus on certain core values led us to an effort to hire more college graduates. We now knew what *great* looked like for us, and college-educated career-minded millennials were an important part of the mix.

Hiring them was challenging, however, because despite great perks, (good pay, reasonable hours, terrific benefits, no required travel), my industry has had trouble attracting and motivating college grads. Some of their objections are unfounded – based on preconceptions that don't hold water – while others are legitimate. We did a deep dive with our college interns to determine why it was tough for us to hire career-minded recent college grads and identified four prime reasons:

- **The stigma of being a car salesperson.** The image in many ways hasn't caught up with the reality, but Jacob himself summed up the preconceptions pretty well recently. His impression of the business, he said, based on no actual interaction, involved "a slick guy with hair greased back, flipping a coin while he waited for you to show up on the lot."
- **The uncertainty of commission-based pay.** This concern, at least for sales positions, is legitimate. As with any commission-based compensation package, ours could be excellent or mediocre depending on sales for any given month. This is a source of frustration for parents who invested heavily in education only to see their children take jobs with uncertain income.
- **Resistance to one-on-one negotiations.** Out of fear, many recent college grads do not like the idea of negotiating with customers on pricing and other details. This has been a fundamental part of the business, and so, is another legitimate objection.
- **Long hours.** Here is another instance where the image has not caught up with the reality. The car business once ground up sales people, but today, a five-day workweek of 46 hours or so is typical – better than most jobs with comparable pay and benefits.

Once I understood the four main barriers to hiring a Jacob – a career-minded college-educated millennial – I set out to design a new position that would address them. The position, like most everything we were doing then, would also have to involve a Written Repeatable Process and address the deep marketplace changes being wrought by the Internet and shifting consumer preferences. Most important, it would have to be built on our core values. In short, the new position I contemplated was a tall and risky order because it went straight to the heart of our business model and the future of our industry.

We named the position we developed "Product Specialist." People in this role would become experts on our products and act as consumer advocates, more like the "Mac Geniuses" found at Apple stores than traditional car salespeople. Product Specialists would not engage in price negotiation or actual sales, so the salesperson stigma and the objection to negotiation were removed. The pay would not involve commission, but a steady salary, with bonuses tied to the number of product demonstrations – not to sales. The long hours had already disappeared, as I mentioned, so we did not need to address that issue, simply make clear the existing expectations.

Once we felt confident that we could remove the objections of a Jacob to our business, we began formulating a handbook for this position, one that would guarantee a Written Repeatable Process. The handbook described in detail the requirements for Product Specialists. They had to be clean-cut, career-minded, college educated, jovial, customer-facing, etc. We also laid out all of the Product Specialists' duties, the necessary education and training, the pay scale, and a well-defined career track, which included the education and production requirements needed to rise to the next level. Our handbook also emphasized the most important overall requirement – people in this role had to reflect and convey our core values.

Perhaps the best test of the Product Specialist position, which was really part of a new business model, was Jacob himself. His father was friends with Keith, the very able general manager of my Lillington store. Keith knows potential when he sees it, and offered Jacob a commission-based sales job when Jacob moved back to North Carolina after briefly working in Michigan. Keith knew that Jacob was the kind of employee we wanted – smart, educated, motivated, friendly, and clean-cut.

The job on offer when Jacob first moved back, however, was a traditional sales job, and he turned it down. His reasons mapped perfectly with the general objections of college-educated millennials that I was working to address. He had worked in sales and marketing in Michigan and did not want to get back on the "rollercoaster" of another commission job, he later told me. He did not want to be "a sales guy." The idea of negotiating pricing and features did not appeal to him. He wanted a way to help people and make a difference in peoples' lives in a career that he felt he had a future.

I was working on the Product Specialist concept when Keith made Jacob that offer. A couple of months later, as we rolled out the program, Keith made another offer to Jacob, explaining the new position. Jacob accepted, becoming part of one of our first classes of product Specialists.

If Jacob was any indication, we had correctly identified the key objections that career-minded college-educated millennials had to entering our business, and created a position that addressed them in a way that would attract the talent we needed. That talent and our new Product Specialist position would be a major step forward in addressing the industry transformation driven by the Internet. We now had the roadmap to offer a new level of service and a new way of purchasing products for consumers who didn't like the old model. We had a way to differentiate ourselves from the competition and look to the future.

Do I sound like I was excited about this program? Jacob sure thought so.

"When the owner of the company interviews you, that says something about how seriously he takes the program," Jacob later told me. (Yes, I interviewed him, and most Product Specialists, myself after the initial manager interviews.) "Your excitement when you first interviewed me was a big factor. That helped reel me in because I could see the energy and excitement in your eyes."

If Jacob perceived the excitement in my eyes during that interview, he no doubt saw the frustration and fear that filled them in the parking lot as he acknowledge that he was leaving – or as he put it, *why I'm not saying*.

A PROMISE AND A 2ND CHANCE

I was bothered by Jacob's impromptu list of the eight problems he'd experienced with the position, maybe even a little angry, though I wasn't sure where to direct that anger. I was most definitely embarrassed. We had worked our tails off to create this job, to hire a Jacob. It all seemed to be working beautifully and now I was being blindsided.

It would have been easy to blame Jacob. Okay, he had seemed like the perfect candidate, but he just wasn't cutting it. I could have seen his list as eight excuses and sent him on his way. I could have blamed a manager or the position itself. *Well, we gave this a shot, but it's much easier to go back to doing things the way they've always been done…*

But I also felt a glimmer of recognition as Jacob listed the eight problems that our Product Specialists faced. I wasn't going to fix this situation by blaming anyone, I quickly understood. If I was going to fix *it*, I had to *fix me first*. This, as you'll see throughout this book, is one of my mantras – a key to success not just in business, in my opinion, but also in marriage, parenting, and relationships of all kinds.

Instead of laying blame or brushing off Jacob's concerns as we sat in an office at our Lillington store, I made a promise.

"Listen, everything you've said I agree with and believe," I started. "I know that to make this program successful, I'm going to have to change these things. I realize you have family commitments, but I really need you to give me a chance here and to help me make these changes to our organization, so that this program works. I need you to help me see it through."

Jacob gave a weighty shrug and looked from the office where we sat across the parking lot. He'd made up his mind and given notice – never an easy task, but especially not in your early twenties – after a few rocky months. He had told his sister he would move to help her, and now, I was asking him to reconsider.

"Look, you're not going to see many chances this early in your career where the owner of the company wants your help in making changes," I said. "Will you at least sit down and walk me through this? I want to hear what you have to say and make sure I understand these problems."

Jacob smiled then, for the first time since I'd stopped him – partly flattered and probably more than a little relieved that I was finally letting him go.

"Yes sir," he said. "Of course."

I did not know at that point if Jacob would stay with the company, but I knew that if I wanted him to answer yes to my question – *will you stay?* – he would have to answer yes to four questions of his own:

- **Do I matter / bring value?**
- **Am I heard? Do I have a voice?**
- **Am I growing and developing?**
- **Am I fairly compensated?**

Decades in business have shown me again and again that these are *the* central questions when it comes to employee engagement. When team members can wholeheartedly answer yes to these four questions, they are motivated, engaged, and giving a job their all. Answering *no* to any one of these spells trouble for both the team member and the organization. Much of effective management involves figuring out which of the four questions an employee can't answer in the affirmative and addressing the surrounding issues.

In Jacob's case, he couldn't answer *yes* to the first three questions. As his list of eight problems hinted, he was being used as a gopher or a sales assistant, which told him that he didn't matter. There is nothing wrong with being a sales assistant, but when you've been hired for a position with more responsibility and then spend your days filling gas tanks and shuttling cars around, the implicit message is that you do not matter.

It wasn't in Jacob's nature to make a fuss, but whatever feedback he was giving about his job and the role of the Product Specialist was obviously falling on deaf ears. He was not being heard. Jacob expected to grow in this job because his initial training was good, but it stopped the second he moved to a store to begin actual work as a Product Specialist. He was no longer learning, or at least not much, and he did not see any semblance of the upward career path we had described when hiring him.

These Four Fundamentals are so essential to my conceptions of employee engagement that at that initial meeting, I was already beginning to address them. Jacob didn't feel like he mattered? Well, he certainly knew he mattered now: the owner of the company was counting on him to help change something that he was passionate about. He wasn't being heard? I was remedying that by being all ears once we sat down together. Jacob hadn't been growing and his training stopped? If we were going to fix that, what could be better than getting one-on-one direction from the company's patriarch?

I hoped that by the end of our meeting, Jacob would be starting to answer *yes* to the first three questions, which were where his problems seemed to lie. As far as I could tell, compensation was not an issue. Many leaders are surprised to learn that this is typical. Good compensation is a trophy for job well done. It's not unimportant and my team members are generally better compensated than their peers at other organizations, but this is the least important of the four key questions. Team members care most about their personal *why* and how it connects to the organization's *why*. *Do I matter? Does my job matter? Am I, and are we, helping people, serving people, serving the community? Is there a clear way for me to grow personally and professionally at this organization?*

These are the important questions and as Jacob later confirmed, they were at the heart of his departure. The questions that burned in my mind as I watched him drive off related directly to the future of my business. Where exactly had I gone wrong with the Product Specialist position and with this hire? Why was a program that seemed perfect on paper failing so miserably in execution? Could I correct the problems Jacob highlighted? Could I offer a new kind of service that made sense in the Internet age and differentiate my organization from the competition? Could I offer a new kind of experience for a new kind of consumer with talented new team members? Jacob very clearly mattered for our organization. In a way, he was its future, but could we keep him?

Finding the answers to those questions would require a lot of listening on my part. I believe that active listening and a special kind of engagement form the foundation of good leadership. I have been working at this kind of leadership for many years, and it has been the key ingredient in whatever success I have enjoyed not only as the owner of a company, but also as a husband, father, friend, and community member. It is perhaps the most valuable thing you can take from this book, and, as I'll document in the next chapter, it all began with a lesson taught to me be a seven-year-old.

THE TAKEAWAYS

- Organizational growth requires effective management strategies – solid systems and tools – if quality service and products are to be maintained.
- Establishing a mission statement, core values, and consistent training builds cohesion, making it possible to manage many employees and multiple locations effectively.
- A focus on Written Repeatable Process allows organizations to move from being talent-oriented to being process-oriented.
- Even a well-conceived program, position, or initiative will fail if you do not have full buy-in from middle management and engagement from frontline employees.
- Employees must answer yes to these 4 fundamental questions to be engaged:
  o Do I matter / bring value?
  o Am I heard? Do I have a voice?
  o Am I growing and developing?
  o Am I fairly compensated?
- The default mindset for effective leadership is: *fix me first*. Most employee failure and disengagement can be traced back to leadership's poor communication or failure to convey the *why* behind tasks.

EXERCISE: FIND YOUR JACOB

I can walk into any organization anywhere – a restaurant, a convenience store, a nonprofit – and tell you in about thirty seconds exactly which employees are engaged and which ones aren't. So can you if you slow down and watch people working. The following exercise will help you hone this skill.

1. Set aside a part of a day to observe workers at your organization.
2. Without being obvious, make an effort to pay attention to various team members going about their daily tasks. Look at body language and facial expressions. Consider tone of voice, energy levels, patience, and irritability. We all frown when something goes wrong, but the employee who spends more time scowling than smiling has a bigger problem than the usual daily hurdles. Drooping shoulders, a tense tone, short answers, a glazed look often point to a lack of engagement and not just a mood or personality issue.
3. As you observe team members, find your Jacob – the talented employee whose engagement level is slipping.
4. Sit down with this person to find out what their concerns are. Spend at least half an hour with them and do more listening than talking. Ask what issues frustrate them at work on a daily basis. What obstacles prevent them from doing a good job? What pitfalls prevent them and the organization from reaching full potential?

As in the case of Jacob, you are likely to get pat answers at first or an insistence that everything is fine. Probe deeper for the real answers. Encourage them to be honest and keep the Four Fundamentals of Employee Engagement firmly in your mind as you talk. Would your team member answer these four questions affirmatively and if not, how can you turn a *no* into a *yes*?

- **Do I matter / bring value?**
- **Am I heard? Do I have a voice?**
- **Am I growing / developing?**
- **Am I fairly compensated?**

CHAPTER 2
Listening And Leading

The Amanda Story: A 7-year-old teaches me the most powerful leadership lesson I have ever learned

Around seventeen years ago, shortly before I started my own business, my oldest daughter, Amanda, brought home a piece of artwork that upset me. She was seven years old at the time, and her second-grade class had made colorful paper turkeys for Thanksgiving. The kids were supposed to write one thing that they were thankful for on each of the turkey's feathers. The first feather on Amanda's turkey noted that she was thankful for God. The second one offered thanks for her Mom, the third for her grandparents, the fourth one for her toys, and so on.

Cute, right? What's so upsetting about that?

Well, there were plenty of feathers on that cutout bird, but her Dad wasn't listed on any of them. Before you think that I was simply vain or too sensitive about a childish oversight, I should explain that Amanda's art project instantly embodied for me a deteriorating relationship with my daughter.

The turkey was particularly painful because, no question about it, Amanda had always been Daddy's girl. We were close from the day she was born. One of the first words she spoke was "Dad." When she was scared, she cried for Daddy. When she had to decide who to ride home with from a restaurant, it was always Daddy. The first stories she penned when learning to write were about adventures with her Dad, and when she learned to draw, her first pictures were of the two of us doing things together.

As a little girl, Amanda would not go to bed until I got home at night, even though I worked late. When she learned how to make phone calls, she would call me at work after school let out, just to chat. We had the kind of bond parents dream of.

At some point, in her seventh year, though, things began to change. A distance crept between us, and our relationship was not quite what it used to be. Amanda stopped waiting up for me to get home. In fact, if she was around when I came home, half the time she would continue playing, without even looking up to say hello. She did not tell me things the way she used to, and the ease that had always marked our interactions disappeared.

Like most dads, I'm less than objective when it comes to my kids, but Amanda really was an angelic child – dark-haired with brown eyes, and a beautiful smile. She got good grades and was well behaved. She was a budding athlete, representing her school in jump-rope competitions, an interest that would later expand into swimming, volleyball, and basketball.

Her strong character was obvious even at seven. I recall one time when a bunch of kids were hanging out at my house and a neighbor spied Amanda alone in the backyard. She asked my daughter what she was doing. Amanda replied that she was "just hanging out," and the neighbor wondered why she wasn't off playing with the other kids.

"I'm not allowed to play by the lake," Amanda said.

"Well, neither are they!" my neighbor replied.

Amanda had self-discipline and did the right thing not out of fear of getting in trouble, but because she knew what good was and wanted to pursue it. That was who she was. But the fact that Amanda was such a good kid only made the growing distance between us harder to bear. I had sensed that my connection to my daughter was fading, but her

Thanksgiving art project confirmed my suspicions and convinced me that I had to do something.

Around that time, I happened to be reading a magazine article that asked the question, what makes people charming? The writer asked readers to consider someone in their lives who was truly charming and to ponder what that person was like. One of the most common traits of charming people, the author asserted, is that they make you feel as if you are the most important person in the room. If your neighbor Dave is charming, it's likely that when you bump into him at the mailbox, he maintains eye contact as you chat, fully focused on you. Cars might be zooming passed, wind blowing, horns honking, but Dave's concentration never lags.

Not only does he listen completely as you talk, he probably remembers your previous conversations and asks about a work issue you described, a recent trip you took, or your child's upcoming graduation. Those little details, perhaps dropped months ago, matter to him, and he cares enough about you to remember them and to ask for updates. In short, he makes you feel like you are one of the most important things in his life.

As I read this article, I thought about my relationship with my daughter. When she was very young and we went to parties, the kids usually played in one room and parents gathered in another. I always went off and played with the kids because I wanted to be present for my children – even if that meant missing out on fun with the adults. In retrospect, I could see that this was one reason that my daughter and I had been so close back then.

Was I still making that kind of effort? Was I still present for Amanda in the same way? I recalled the conversations we'd had during the previous six months, or at least I tried to. The truth is, not a single meaningful conversation came to mind. There was a lot of her asking for things and me saying no. There was a lot of me correcting, directing, and disciplining her, but little real talking. I had to do something to change this situation, but what?

LEARNING TO LISTEN

The same day that I realized I couldn't think of a recent substantive conversation that I'd had with Amanda, I called my wife from work. I told her that when I got home, I wanted her to take our other daughter, Ashley, who was three at the time, so that I could spend some time alone with Amanda. My wife understood the struggle I was having and so, of course, was more than willing. You see, I had sensed this issue months earlier and sought advice from a variety of people. Everyone had an opinion – and none of them was right.

"Amanda, can you and I go talk?" I asked when I arrived home from work that evening.

"Am I in trouble?"

"No, I just wanted to talk to you honey," I said, as mildly as I could. "I haven't really talked to you in a while."

"Okay," she said warily and, shrugging, she followed me into her room.

"How was your day?" I asked.

"Fine. Why, did something happen?" she asked, alarm overcoming suspicion in her tone.

I assured her that nothing had happened and that she hadn't done anything wrong. I asked her once again how her day had been. "Fine," she repeated. I asked her about homework – she didn't have any. She shrugged and shook her head when I wondered if she'd learned anything interesting or done anything fun at school that day. A silence thick as fog rose between us.

"Can I go now?" she finally asked and, seeing how uncomfortable she was, I let her.

I left the room dejected. My plan had failed miserably, but I still felt that I was onto something. I had supplemented that magazine article on charming people with a book that offered a similar take. Its author asked readers if they'd ever been in a restaurant and spotted that young couple across the room, the guy who's hanging on the edge of his seat and the woman who's perched on upright on hers as they lock eyes, each devouring the other's every gesture and word. The rest of the room, of the world even, doesn't seem to exist for them. They are searching for mutual interests and similar experiences, something they can build on.

First date is the usual guess, right? The couple are trying to put their best foot forward, to find common ground, to really understand each other. They ask a million questions and call on an abundance of empathy, building a foundation that could be the basis for a relationship.

"How about that other couple?" the author of the book I was reading asked next. Have you ever noticed the pair who seem to be at different tables, though they're sitting two feet apart? She's checking her cell phone or looking over his shoulder, while he's glued to the TV or distracted by a waitress. They talk past each other, if at all, as if they long ago said everything there was to say. *They've been married forever,* you think, right?

I kept this example in mind as I continued trying to get closer to Amanda. A few days after my first attempt, I called my wife and again asked if she would take Ashley so that I could spend some time with Amanda when I got home. Once again, my daughter and I slumped into her room, both feeling painfully self-conscious. Again I asked about her day, and once again, she was uncomfortable and evasive, though maybe slightly less so than the first time. At least now she knew that she wasn't in trouble and that there was no ulterior agenda – Dad, weirdo that he was, really did just want to talk.

As I undertook these efforts, I continued my reading. Everything I came across pointed to the conclusion that, at that stage of my life, I was not a great listener. On top of this deficiency, my boss had been diagnosed with cancer, so I had been working a lot, away from home for longer and longer stretches. It would have been easy to blame Amanda or those tumultuous childhood years for our lack of connection and go on with business as usual: *Kids...just a phase...it's a tough time... she'll snap out of it.* I was tempted to hold her responsible, but such excuses didn't ring true. Everything I felt and read seemed to suggest that some if not most of this was on me.

I decided to continue my strategy, to work at listening, to sit upright on the edge of my seat, and to do whatever I could to correct course. I would continue to invest in my relationship with Amanda even if I felt awkward and out of place.

A BREAKTHROUGH

The next week, when I was in Amanda's room, trying once again to engage with her, I mentioned that Phillip, a guy I worked with (and who works with me to this day), had driven a car into a wall at the dealership. Amanda knew Phillip and she knew Daryl, our boss at the time.

"Oh my gosh," she said. "Did he get in trouble?" A spark of interest flared in her eyes, which instantly widened.

"Yeah, he got in big trouble," I said. "You know how Daryl is."

"Did he get hurt?" she asked

"Well, he was okay. The thing that really got hurt was his pride."

"Oh gosh," she said, no doubt feeling bad for Phillip. "Well, what happened after he did it?"

I explained what happened after the accident, and she asked another question about the repercussions. As I answered her I had to bite my tongue to keep from smiling, to remain casual and matter-of-fact. We were, I realized, enjoying a full-blown conversation, the first one I'd had with my daughter in some time.

A few minutes later, she began telling me about this little kid who had pushed her on the playground at school. Again it was difficult not to react negatively. The first thing you want to do when you hear about a person bothering or hurting your child is look for someone to beat up, but I made a conscious effort to simply listen, with all of my attention fixed on her. If I spoke during her story, it was only to ask a question or draw her out.

We had a great conversation that day, and before each of the next several times that we sat down together, I thought of other stuff that was happening at work or in my life generally to tell Amanda – things that I normally would have considered too trivial to mention. My opening up to her and sharing prompted her to share more with me, and she was encouraged because she could see that I was listening completely, giving her my full and sincere attention. I left no room for doubt: she was *the* most important thing in the room, in the house, in my life in those moments.

Soon, Amanda was not only waiting up for me, she was calling me at work to see what time I'd be home and to ask if we could talk when I got in. Within a matter of weeks, our relationship went from nearly non-existent to stronger than ever.

A couple of weeks later, as Christmas approached, my wife and I were headed to Greensboro. I had won a weekend at the Grandover from a contest, and there were a host of planned events. Lisa, called me at work and asked what I was going to do on that Saturday when we were away. I was planning on golfing, I said. Oh, okay, she said, no problem.

"Why, what did you have in mind?" I asked.

"Oh, nothing really," she said. "Don't worry about it."

I asked again why she'd checked about Saturday because in the back of my mind I'd been thinking, my efforts with Amanda were working so well, maybe I should take this weekend in Greensboro and try the same strategy with my wife. Lisa said she'd thought maybe we could finish our Christmas shopping, but then quickly repeated that it was no big deal and I should have fun golfing.

"No," I said, "let's go shopping. Let's knock this out."

"No," she said. "You want to golf. Go. Have fun."

I told her that it was going to be cold, and I didn't really want to golf anyway. I would rather go shopping with her. She demurred, but I insisted until we finally agreed to buy the last of our presents. My wife and I, I should say here, had a great relationship and a strong marriage, but after all my reading and my talks with Amanda, I wondered if it could be even better. Lisa really was the most important person in the room for me, always, but was I showing her that adequately?

The mall seemed like the perfect place to test such questions because my wife loves to shop. Actually, she's a pretty good shopper the way Tom Brady is a pretty good quarterback. Somewhere at corporate headquarters, American Express has a plaque with her smiling face on it. Deciding that the two of us would do something that she loves was a good first step.

I left the planning to her. She wanted to start shopping on Friday and finish up on Saturday. Lisa and I arrived at the mall early that first day and stopped for a cup of coffee, to gear up. As we sat down in the coffee shop, I kept the strategies I'd been using with Amanda at the front of my mind. I was becoming a better listener, and I consciously focused on everything my wife had to say. *Okay, John,* I said to myself, *sit on the edge of your seat. Concentrate. Give her ALL of your attention. No glancing at the TV or your phone. Make sure that Lisa knows she is the most important person in the room.*

As with Amanda, I shared things from work and other parts of my life that I would normally have thought too mundane to bring up. I asked Lisa about her day and her week. One question led to another, one answer to another, and two hours later, we were still sitting there, with rapt attention. We perched on the edges of our seats, eyes locked, hanging on every gesture and word. The rest of the room, the world, didn't exist for us. After years of marriage, we had become that first-date couple once again. The conversation turned out to be one of the best we'd had in a long time, so good that my wife the professional shopper no longer even wanted to enter a store. A random weekend when I was supposed to go golfing and we instead decided to do some shopping became perhaps the best weekend we'd had up to that point.

LESSONS LEARNED

What I learned from using these strategies to reestablish my connections to my wife and daughter is that the relationships in your life are almost completely – 95 percent, if not 100 percent – in your control. Nearly everything that happens to you is a reaction to something that you put in play, an idea that can be a source of both great comfort and anxiety. Comfort because if things aren't going well, fixing them is almost always within your power. Anxiety because, since you *can* fix those problems, you no longer have pat excuses or easy outs to fall back on. My daughter has grown distant? I can't blame a "phase" or pre-teen moodiness. That's on me now, a responsibility that can be troubling. My spouse and I no longer connect? Only I can change the situation, and the solution starts, as I have said before and will repeat throughout the book, with *fixing me first*.

This isn't a book about parenting or marriage, but as you've probably guessed by now, the same principles that I've been describing apply to managing team members and running a business or any organization. Just as Amanda hadn't really changed when we grew distant, your disengaged team member probably hasn't changed either. If this was the right person when you hired them, they are probably still that person, so begin by asking what you might have done or not done to cause a change.

I began replicating at work the same techniques I'd used with Amanda, and achieved the same stellar results. It turns out that the same qualities that make for good parenting also make for good leaders. Let's think about those traits that good parents share, spelling out the things that my story about Amanda illustrate. Good parents:

- **Listen well**
- **Are mindful of body language**
- **Stay engaged**
- **Share what's happening in their lives**

- **Sacrifice time and attention**
- **Know that the relationship is in their control**

Team members, like children, generally want to do good. They want to produce great work. Most problems occur because *they don't know what great looks like.* That lack of a target or standards, the absence of a tangible *why* – the purpose behind a task or objective – usually starts with a communication failure on the leader's part, not the employee's failure, though the default setting is to blame the employee. Rather than passing the buck, it is incumbent on a strong leader to say, I have to *fix me first.*

The model I'm suggesting requires a strong leader to begin by looking inward. Assessing each of the guidelines above, as a good parent might, is the first step. There is a problem with a team member? Before you evaluate her performance, evaluate your own. Have you been truly and actively **listening** to this person, or has her direct supervisor? The mistake that most of us make – and the mistake I made with my daughter and wife – is to think of listening as a passive endeavor. It most definitely is not.

True listening is active, and it's a two-way street. Remember my example of Dave, the charming neighbor who greets you at the mailbox? Dave shows through his **body language** – the way his eyes fix on yours, the way he leans forward, the way he nods and grunts reactions as you speak – that he is hanging on your every word. A natural principle underlies active listening: **if I show that you are important to me, I become important to you.**

Dave asks questions both in response to what you're saying in the moment and to things you mentioned weeks or months ago – the award you won at work, the weekend away with your spouse, your kid's fifth birthday party. His active listening makes you feel that *you matter*, which you'll recall, is the first of our Four Fundamentals of Employee Engagement:

- **Do I matter / bring value?**
- **Am I heard**
- **Am I growing?**
- **Am I fairly compensated?**

While leaders are checking the boxes on the good parenting and managing traits above, assessing their own leadership techniques, they are simultaneously addressing the Four Fundamentals of Employee Engagement. The two work hand in hand, so that a leader who is diligently applying all of those techniques eventually will have team members who can answer *yes* to the Four Fundamentals, who are motivated and engaged – and much easier to lead.

The three traits of good parenting that follow "listen well" are closely related to that first trait and are part and parcel of active listening. A good leader, like a good parent, can read volumes from body language. Looking is a part of active listening, too. Slouching shoulders, perpetual frowning, frequent sighs, glassy eyes, evasive looks – all are signs of disengagement. This might all sound obvious, but I have seen endless managers ignore the obvious physical signs of discontent for all sorts of reasons that they can justify: they need the employee, there's no one to replace him or her, they're scared, bringing it up will make them look bad…

Reading body language is a skill like any other, one that emerges naturally from human behavior, though we're often too busy or blind to attend to it. Tackling the exercise at the end of Chapter 1, "Finding your Jacob," is a good way to begin honing this key management skill. If you work at it as I have, you will know within thirty seconds of entering a conference room, the sales floor, or a back office exactly which team members are engaged and which are falling short in one or more of the Four Fundamentals.

Staying engaged, the third trait, also requires practice and persistence. After a couple of awkward meetings with Amanda, it would have been easy for me to say, *oh well, I tried*, and move on. No one wants to sit through painful silences or strained conversations, but those are often the walls we must break through to remain engaged. One attempt at listening becomes meaningless without follow-through and steady interaction. **Sharing** what's happening in your organization – long-term vision, staffing levels, a new advertising direction, planned expansions – is a vital part of that engagement. It makes you appear open and human, and it creates trust.

As a manager, supervisor, or owner, "sharing" does not mean merely shooting the breeze with a team member, though casual conversation can break the ice and build a connection. On a deeper level, "sharing" often requires explaining clearly the larger goals behind a particular job, task, or objective. Team members get motivated when leaders explain the larger purpose, or *why,* behind a position, process, or initiative.

Sharing with a team member the goals of the organization and how the employee's individual contributions will help achieve them, how those contributions relate to the larger core values and core focus, is a powerful way to engage employees. Taking the time to paint the big picture is much more effective than simply giving orders, and it's perhaps the best way there is to show a team member that he or she matters. *The boss is talking to* me *about strategy and how my work relates to the organization's core values? Maybe my job is more important than I thought...*

A good leader will connect tasks or jobs to the individual's growth as well as to the company's growth, addressing the third of the Four Fundamentals. *Here's how doing a great job on this relates to your career and movement up the ladder.* Team members are much more engaged when they know that there is room to grow and see a clear map for moving up.

I can already hear swamped middle managers sighing at these suggestions (how's that for reading body language?) even if they sound good. Who has time for this, right? Let me suggest that the less time you have, the more important these strategies are. Investing time on the front end means fewer headaches later. It means more motivated and engaged employees with greater longevity at the organization. I won't lie to you – this involves **sacrifice**, a word good parents know well. It takes time and effort and often means stopping what you're doing to listen and to explain, but that sacrifice produces team members who are a joy to manage rather than a struggle. Getting the right skis and poles takes time, money, and effort. It is a sacrifice of sorts, but consider how much harder it is to navigate the slopes without that investment.

The bottom line here is that **the relationship is in your control**. This is true with your spouse or partner, children, friends, and team members. Making the sort of investment that I'm encouraging – actively listening, being aware of body language, staying engaged over the long haul, sharing with team members, and sacrificing when necessary – will make you a better leader, and them better team members. They will feel more inclined to contribute mentally as well as physically. You will be more in tune with your employees and more aware of the roots of problems rather than just their fallout. Your team will be more motivated, which means you can spend more time focused on big-picture goals rather than daily minutiae.

LISTENING TO JACOB

Everything I've described in this chapter sounds simple enough, but in the heat and daily chaos of running an organization the strategies become much more complex. It's easy to stop listening or ignore body language when you have a million things on your plate. *Fixing me first* takes time, which is at a premium for most managers, owners, and executive directors.

One of the reasons that I'm focusing on the story about Jacob in this book is that it demonstrates both the effectiveness of this sort of leadership and the missteps that can occur if you take your eye off the ball. I hired Jacob years after Amanda taught me those lessons on listening, engagement, and leadership, so why didn't I stop at the first sign I saw in his eyes, when I asked his manager about how he was doing? Why was I blindsided and left struggling to understand in that parking lot a key organizational initiative that I initially thought was going well?

In this spirit of *fix me first,* I started by asking myself those questions. What had I done wrong or communicated poorly? After Jacob rattled off the problems with the new Product Specialist position the day that I stopped him in the lot, I realized that I had not adequately shared with my middle managers just how critical this program was. As I explained in Chapter 1, I saw the new role of Product Specialist as existential. The future of my business and industry depended on this kind of forward thinking. It was not a random experiment but a mission-critical initiative.

My middle managers, at least some, had nodded and agreed with the program and supposedly gotten on board, but in reality, they didn't quite get **why** this new person with a funny title was hanging around or why his job was vital for the organization. As Jacob explained to me, they were using him mostly to transport vehicles, fuel them up, set up OnStar, etc. The person who, on paper, was a consumer advocate, demonstrating products and providing information in a revolutionary new way, became in reality a low-level assistant.

I had not adequately conveyed the ways that the Product Specialist program was linked to our health and growth as an organization and to my managers' growth as individuals within the organization. Sure, I said it was "important," maybe even used the word "vital," but I had not truly conveyed the *why* behind the program, which as I argued above, is the great motivator. If I had paid better attention to body language, I might have picked up clues that my managers, at least some, weren't fully on board or did not completely fit our core values.

I also did not stay engaged with those managers as much as I should have. When Amanda insisted that nothing had happened at school and tersely listed the subjects she'd studied the day of our first meeting, I made the space to listen and share week after week until she began opening up and we had good conversations. In retrospect, I could see that I did not show that level of engagement with my middle managers when it came to the Product Specialists. In the movie, *A Few Good Men,* the character of Colonel Jessup explains why in his world, an order is never questioned: *We follow orders or people die.* The same ethos holds true at many organizations, but a good leader must listen to concerns and objections regarding an order if he wants those tasked with carrying it out fully on board.

There are no easy answers when it comes to leadership. Strong leadership requires constant vigilance. I am thankful every day for Amanda's story, but I still have to work at listening and engagement. I regularly have to hit the reset button and remind myself that my relationships with team members are within my control. When I fall short in some way, I know that I can rely on those strategies I began developing as I reconnected with my daughter and wife to fix the situation, which means fixing me first.

After Jacob's first month or so, you'll recall, I did notice body language suggesting that his engagement level was slipping. I brought this up with his direct boss, who assured me everything was fine. I obviously had not done a good enough job instilling my leadership techniques in Jacob's boss. I use those strategies with all of my direct-reports, who I am fully responsible for. Ideally, they should be using the same techniques with their direct reports and so on, throughout the organization.

There was a breakdown in Jacob's case, but I immediately sought him out to listen to what he had to say. The techniques I used in the parking lot and at our subsequent meeting are the same as the ones I learned from Amanda. There was a similar awkwardness and a reluctance on Jacob's part to open up. I hung on his every word, though, and my body language and questions showed him that I was engaged. I shared with him, just as I had with Amanda, by telling him how important his position was to the company and how much I needed his help.

Before Jacob left, he already was beginning to answer yes to the first Fundamental of Employee Engagement: *Do I matter / bring value?* And something that seemed out of my control – an employee quitting to help his sister – turned out to be almost completely in my control. Yes, there was a sister who needed help, but Jacob's departure was really a ripple effect of my communication failure, not of a new baby.

The leadership strategies I'm encouraging in this book are key for motivating employees and remaining competitive. Jacob's story demonstrates both their power and the fact that even with the best of intentions and a solid plan, any leader can fall short. Amid the din and roar of the work week, the countless tasks that need doing and fires that need dousing, it's easy for things to slip. This is why the strategies I'm presenting here need to be built into the organization systemically.

In the following chapters, I'll explore the fundamental tools (some of which I've already mentioned) that allow this sort of leadership to flourish. True leadership thrives when the organization has established core values, clearly defined roles, Written Repeatable Process, and solid verifiable measures. Such leadership creates real accountability and traces problems to their source by instilling a culture of listening, a servant ethos, and managers who always try to "fix me first."

THE TAKEAWAYS

- The relationships in your life are almost completely in your control. Nearly everything affecting you – including employee failures – is a reaction to your actions.
- Effective leaders strengthen relationships and achieve results through active listening and a fix-me-first approach.
- Charming people are active listeners, making you feel you're important, sitting on the edge of their seats, asking questions, focusing, sharing, and staying engaged.
- A natural principle underlies active listening: if you are important to me, I become important to you.
- Good listeners share the traits of good parents. They:
  o Listen well
  o Are mindful of body language
  o Stay engaged
  o Share what's happening in their lives
  o Sacrifice time and attention
  o Know that the relationship is in their control
- Most team failures are really a leader's failure to convey the *why* behind a task, its larger purpose and relation to big goals. This is why leaders must "fix me first."
- Good listening and leadership techniques automatically address the Four Fundamentals of Employee Engagement.
- Top leaders should instill active listening and a fix-me-first approach in all direct reports, who should do the same with theirs, to build a culture of listening and engagement.

EXERCISE: THE CHARMING PERSON

Think of someone in your life who is truly charming. This might be a friend, neighbor, relative, co-worker, boss...

1. Consider the traits that make this person charming. Don't just rely on memory here – do some recon. The next couple of times you interact with this person, pay attention to their body language, tone, eye contact. Notice their reactions when you share something about yourself or your business.

2. Make a mental note of the kinds of questions they ask and the things they share about themselves. Be natural, but approach these conversations with the eye of an anthropologist. You might even jot a few notes after each one.

3. Now think about someone important to you who has felt distant or disengaged. This might be a friend, employee, or someone on your team.

4. Without seeming forced, do your best to emulate the traits of your designated "charming person" during your next three interactions with the disengaged person. Maybe you ask more follow-up questions than normal, share more about yourself, or take extra time to explain how a task is important to a larger organizational strategy. Maintain eye contact, sound interested, be engaged. Don't look at your phone or watch. Remember how important this time is to you.

5. Reflect on how these new interactions change the dynamics of the relationship. What changes do you notice in the other person or the conversation when you talk next time? How might you apply this strategy to other relationships with employees or team members?

CHAPTER 3
Defining Core Values And Roles

You get what you settle for if you don't know what you want

Some years ago, my wife and I bought a house that had many features we liked. There was a spacious ground-level master bedroom and a large kitchen, both big pluses for us. We wanted a view of either water or a golf course, and this home had both. The neighborhood was pleasant and quiet. We moved in happily, but the house was a little older and, we knew, less than perfect.

One day I sat on my porch, thinking about what it would take to make our house perfect. I pulled out my trusty legal pad and began to make a list. I didn't like the patio configuration, partly because the outdoor fireplace faced the wrong direction. I wrote that down and several other things I didn't like about the outdoor space. There were more interior problems – none more annoying than the low water pressure. My girls complained about it constantly. We had four shower heads. None of them had good pressure, and one didn't work at all. I listed this problem, along with several others.

I set the list aside and went about my day, but the next morning when I got my cup of coffee and turned my computer on, as I did most mornings, I looked at my legal pad and thought, what would it take to get great water pressure in my house? I searched online and saw an article about a big expansion tank that could be installed in a crawl space to boost pressure. I wasn't sure if that would work in my house or how much it might cost, so on a whim, I called my plumber friend Troy.

"Troy, listen," I said, "I bought this house about a year ago, and it has no water pressure. Have you ever installed one of these expansion tanks?"

Troy asked if I was on city water. I said that I was, and he asked my address.

"I'm going to be over that way this morning," he said. "If you can hang out a while, I'll swing by."

I told him I'd be there. I didn't know if an expansion tank was feasible, but I hadn't seen Troy in several years and it would be good to catch up regardless.

He arrived that morning and after our hellos, pulled out a little gauge, which he placed on an outdoor spigot. The reading indicated 45 pounds of pressure.

"Where's your crawlspace?" Troy asked.

I walked him over, and he climbed into the crawlspace to reach a little valve, which he turned. We returned to the spigot. The pressure had moved from forty-five to fifty-five pounds.

"Wow," I said. "That was easy. Is there any way we could get a little more?"

"I can go to sixty," he said. "More than that and you could start blowing seals in your appliances."

He returned to the crawlspace and dialed the pressure up to sixty.

"How much do I owe you?" I asked.

"Nothing. It was good to see you again." We visited a few minutes more, and then he left.

I went in the house and tested our showers. Not only did the three that we used daily have great pressure, the one that hadn't worked was back in business after Troy's adjustment.

I felt like a genius and an idiot in the same instant. I was a genius because the adjustment had taken all of ten minutes. It didn't cost a penny, and it would mean a major improvement in our quality of life. My wife and daughters would greet me like a hero after their next showers. I'd eliminated a source of daily complaints and in some small way, the whole house would be happier.

I was also an idiot. We had lived there for a full year with rotten water pressure. A lake view is nice, but bathing is how you start you day. It wakes you up and sets the tone for your morning. It's fundamental, not a frill, and we'd suffered poor showers all this time when a simple phone call and a free ten-minute adjustment could have eliminated a major source of inconvenience. I had settled for poor water pressure because I didn't take the time to decide what I wanted.

DETERMINING CORE VALUES

As you know by now if you've read the previous two chapters, this story, too, has big implications for how you run your business or organization. The subtitle of this chapter is drawn from my water pressure story, and it's become something of an aphorism for me, one my managers are intimately familiar with: *You get what you settle for if you don't know what you want.* Did my family know on some level that we wanted great water pressure, in the same way that you know you want great employees? Of course, but it wasn't until I sat down and wrote out a list of what *great* would look like and set priorities that I realized how important it was, and found a path to get it. Before that, I was settling, which is what even the smartest leaders tend to do under the daily pressures of running an organization.

You can't get what you want until you know what you want. This sounds obvious, but an enormous number of problems at organizations arise because team members don't know *what great looks like.* When the direction is not clear, we do what *we think* is important. Unfortunately, what we think is often wrong if leaders have not taken the time to decide and / or to communicate clearly what they want, what "great" means for the organization and the individual.

In Chapter 1, I mentioned briefly that defining our core values was a game changer for my business and was critical to a shift in organizational culture. Here, I want to delve deeper into core values and suggest that readers should think about them initially as simply deciding in broad terms what they want. What do you value as an organization? Is it selling the greatest number of widgets to the greatest number of consumers? Is it being number one in your industry or the top supplier of a particular service in your city? Is it being 100 percent reliable or the fastest at what you do? Is it creativity, resourcefulness, always going the extra mile for clients? If you're a nonprofit, maybe it involves providing the most holistic services possible to homeless clients or performing every task with compassion and understanding.

There is no right answer. No two organizations have exactly the same set of core values, and they shouldn't. Core values must emerge organically from what *you* want as an organization, what great looks like for *your* team and *your* clients.

Look, some readers will say, everyone we deal with, customers and employees, know that honesty or thrift or smart solutions or – fill in the blank – is paramount for us. I don't need to announce it on a bumper sticker. But deciding on core values isn't about creating wall art. It's easy to take that superficial approach. What I'm talking about is quite different, something fundamental to your organization and its culture. Doing the hard work to decide on your true core values ultimately helps you hire, fire, train, strategize, manage, advertise...Done properly, a core values initiative seeps into every fiber of your business. Core values become a part of every decision, the thing that differentiates you, and the rudder that steers the ship, helping you navigate tough waters.

As someone who suffered a year of poor water pressure and ran my business for nearly a decade before formally establishing core values, let me assure you, *writing down* what great looks like makes all the difference. It wasn't until I made my list on the front porch that I realized how much my family valued water pressure. Once I wrote it into a list and determined what great looked like for us, I got exactly what I wanted. I have seen this again and again in business, too: decide what you want, what great looks like, and a way forward appears. Fail to clearly define and write out your core values, and settling becomes your organizational M.O.

How do leaders go about determining an organization's core values? I'm glad you asked. I will run through the process I used, which roughly follows the steps outlined in an excellent book called *Traction: Get a Grip on Your Business*, by Gino Wickman. I highly recommend this book if you want to delve deeper into the process and get Wickman's take.

My basic approach combined the lessons I have learned about leadership and listening over the years with a *Traction* exercise. I set aside an entire day, or most of one, and as a company, we gathered our seven key managers in a room. As Wickman advises, we asked each of these leaders to identify three stellar team members within the organization. These are the people who, if you could clone them, would allow you to dominate your industry, ideal, inspirational employees. They could come from any part of the business – salesperson, receptionist, delivery driver, etc. – though I asked my managers to avoid naming people in the room (we didn't want a back-patting session). In small organizations, it's also fine to look outside of your business to find the three model team members. A past peer or leader can work nicely.

We put the names up on a board. There was some overlap. We eliminated duplicates, so we had about fourteen in total after everyone had chosen three. Next, following Wickman's guidelines, we asked, why did you pick this person? What were the characteristics that prompted you to put him or her on your list? As with listing the ideal team members, there was some overlap of characteristics, but finally we probably had forty traits in total on the board.

There was a wide range of answers, as you can imagine. They included things like: impeccable character, gets it done, always does what she says, puts other people before himself, problem-solver, mission-minded…

Of these characteristics, we then asked, which ones are the most important to be a part of our organization? We debated and discussed, and whittled the list down to the most important twenty, then ten, and finally five. You need everyone to be honest for this to work. If you cut people off or talk over them, you will not get it right.

This discussion is a key part of the process because every organization is different and will value different qualities. *Great* at my organization will look at least a little different from *great* at yours, and maybe a whole lot different. You have to be honest here and choose the qualities you truly value as a team. If "aggressively competitive" or "takes no prisoners" or "puts winning first" is what you want as an organization, don't choose "cares for others" as a core value. Don't pick my core values just so that you can hang a pleasant plaque in reception. You are discussing who you are as a team and the qualities that will propel you forward. This is not about public relations.

The other key piece of advice I have, drawing on the Amanda story, in Chapter 2, is make sure that everyone in the room has a voice and is listened to. Being listened to is a key part of feeling that you matter, that you are heard, and that you have room to grow and develop – the three most important of our Four Fundamentals of Engagement – and it's vital to have your leaders buy into this effort. They will be the people on the frontlines, instilling these core values throughout the organization. The process has to be open and collaborative, and if your managers don't buy in it becomes a futile exercise.

WHY THESE 5 VALUES?

My managers and I had a spirited, illuminating discussion as we explored the traits listed on the board. By the end of the whole process, which lasted about six hours, we had the five core values that our organization would live and die by. Here they are, in no particular order:

- **Character and integrity**
- **Professional**
- **Servant attitude**
- **Loves people**
- **Get-it-done attitude**

As you can see, some items on our list are not surprising, but overall, it is fairly idiosyncratic. If you saw it in isolation, you probably would not guess *sales organization*. Let's look at them briefly, one by one:

Character and integrity probably appear an easy pick, and yes, many businesses would say they value this trait, but you would be surprised how many sales organizations would not rate it in their top twenty, much less their top five. For us, it's a no-brainer. We want to surround ourselves with people who have a high degree of character and integrity because so many other fine qualities begin there. We only want people who are going to do what they say they will do. When they make a mistake, we want them to own it, even if it's something that might cost the company money.

Professional is another obvious one. As leaders, we realized that having employees interact with and respond to customers in a professional manner – always courteous and helpful, knowledgeable, and great at their jobs – is a high priority for our organization. We want people who try to hone their craft and be the very best at what they do. Even dressing and looking professional is important to us, whereas a music store or nightclub might cultivate a very different aesthetic.

Servant attitude might be more surprising. It would be an obvious choice for a church group, but it was near the top for us, too. As we wrote out the key qualities of the people we wanted to clone, we realized that they consistently put others before themselves. They had a kind of servant's attitude, and I suppose that's no accident. I started this company, and my go-to example of leadership has always been the story of Jesus demonstrating servant-leadership by getting down on the ground to wash his disciples' feet. True leaders serve, I believe, and they operate with a kind of humility that very much aligns with the "fix-me-first" attitude I am encouraging.

This notion of a "servant attitude" – an urge to help customers at all costs and put others first – was something I'd always felt in my gut, or my heart more accurately, but never spelled out, not even to myself. I felt an incredible epiphany sitting in that room as my managers helped me come to the conclusion that for me and for our organization, this was a key part of what great looks like.

Loves people stirred the same sense of revelation when my managers and I all said that we treasured this quality in our best team members. Together in our core values session, we explored what we meant by this and agreed that we appreciated those with a deep-seated love of people, not just pleasant people or high-performers or smart people, but *all* people. You see, love is meant to be unconditional, not based on *what's in it for me*. Therefore, we think that counseling or reprimanding someone is vital because it's in the best interest of the employee, just as it would be in the best interest of your child.

We want team members who love their peers and subordinates. If you love people, that generally means that you're happy to be around those you work with and for, and those who you manage. It also means that you care enough about people and their futures to stop production in order to correct a problem and put them back on the correct path. In our management model, love is the basis for stopping the daily workflow in order to encourage someone or to reprimand him or her if a behavior or action is not in the team member's best interest for the future.

Get-it-done attitude is another trait that I have always valued and, in fact, touted but never wrote down or named a "core value." Thinking back to the very first employee I hired when we started the company (a guy who's still with us, by the way), I loved the fact that he never cared about who was responsible for a problem in the moment, only about the best possible way to solve it for the customer or employee. Figuring out who *should've* or *could've* was for after the issue was resolved and we could effect change.

USING YOUR CORE VALUES

As I hope you can sense from the description of my organization's experience above, simply going through the process of establishing core values is enlightening. It forces you to choose what's really important to you, which is another way of saying, it forces you to define what great looks like. Once you've named that thing and written it down – whether it's great water pressure or a servant attitude – paths to achieving it begin to present themselves. If you put your heart into this endeavor, I can guarantee that your management team will emerge reinvigorated, with a new sense of mission and motivation.

Core values are about far more than stoking mangers, however. At my organization, we immediately began hiring and firing based on our shared core values. We used to hire based on talent, as I mentioned in Chapter 1. You had a great sales record, went to the best accounting school, had an impressive resume, were an expert mechanic – okay, you were in. Not anymore. We didn't ignore talent, but as we interviewed candidates, we cared far more about their alignment with our core values.

An applicant might have been the best salesperson in ten states, but if she didn't have a "servant attitude" we weren't interested. You're a top-notch finance guy with years of experience, but you don't love people? Sorry, you're barking up the wrong business. We began talking in-depth about our core values during interviews. They gave our managers powerful new criteria for considering candidates and gave potential employees a much clearer picture of who we were and what we wanted. To some, the list sounded like heaven, and to others, not so much.

We also realized early on that core values were not just a tool for hiring and firing. They required us to take a hard look at our current employees, too, to ensure they were aligned with these standards. If they fell short on a core value and wanted to work at getting up to speed, we were happy to help them do that. If they were unable or unwilling to align with our core values, we pointed out amicably that it's much easier to find a job when you have a job and that they should probably get ready to move on.

Core values became a central part of all training for new team members and our primary measurement tool as we conducted our quarterly evaluations. Employees quickly came to understand that they would be dismissed far more quickly for a core values infraction than for any other issue.

Thinking of a core values effort simply as a way to post something on the office wall is like framing the Marshall Plan as a way to spruce up some damaged buildings in Europe. For my organization, establishing and using core values in the ways that I'm outlining became the cornerstone of a dramatic cultural change.

I alluded to this change in Chapter 1, when I wrote that we moved from a talent-driven organization to a process-driven one. A focus on talent gets you some skilled team members, no doubt about it, and they often achieve strong results. It's like a drug that makes you feel good for a while, but next thing you know, you're a prisoner to it. Your business is experiencing rollercoaster highs and lows rather than sustainable growth. It was difficult for me to let go of some talented employees who didn't share our core values, but in every instance, the rest of the team worked more effectively and cohesively once that person was gone, and our overall results improved.

A group of like-minded people working in harmony is more successful than individuals marching to different beats, no matter how talented some of them are. Focusing on our core values and prioritizing process over talent also meant less turnover. Like-minded team members with shared values tend to stay at an organization much longer. And any leader can relate to the fact that longevity tends to mean fewer headaches and easier management. We had grown as a talent-based organization, but our growth was much healthier, more consistent, and more profitable once we became process-driven and focused on our core values. It was steadier because it had less to do with talented individuals having a good month, then a bad month, and more to do with a cohesive team supporting each other within a process they understood and contributed to.

DEFINE ROLES UPFRONT

As the patriarch of the company, establishing core values and shifting organizational culture helped me to strategize, too. As I looked to solve problems and plan for our future, I constantly turned core values over in my mind. We now understood as an organization what *great* looked like. We had clear targets, which eliminated many applicants and pointed us toward particular pools of employees, including an additional demographic – college-educated career-minded millennials. The Product Specialist position was an outgrowth of our focus on core values and our exploration of who we could add to the team to help us demonstrate them.

Hiring these additional team members, however, would be a challenge. I touched on this process in Chapter 1, explaining the trouble our industry has had attracting college grads and the research we did to determine the main obstacles. Why did they not look at our industry as the great opportunity it is? We narrowed it down to these four things:

- **The stigma of being a car salesperson**
- **The uncertainty of commission-based pay**
- **Resistance to one-on-one negotiations**
- **Long hours**

While I was thinking of ways to recruit career-minded college-educated millennials by removing these roadblocks, we were also trying to address a changing sales environment heavily influenced by the Internet. The strategies I considered for addressing these two issues all rested on our core values.

I came up with one answer to both challenges by creating the Product Specialist position that we hired Jacob and others to fill. Product Specialists, as I've noted, had to be clean-cut, college educated, jovial, customer-facing, etc. They would operate more like the "Mac Geniuses" at Apple stores than traditional sales people – highly knowledgeable about the product and paid by salary, not commission. They would be consumer advocates, always available and eager to help, but without ever having to negotiate.

We not only created the idea of this new position, we clearly spelled out a detailed description of the qualities and qualifications that candidates should have and crafted a handbook for the job. Here is another example of why it's vital to *know what great looks like*. Managers in our organization understand that in every instance, for every single hire, they must create a detailed profile of the ideal candidate – defining *great* – before they even place an ad. If you don't define the roles thoroughly upfront, you will settle for what comes through the door, oftentimes justifying attempts to squeeze round pegs into square holes.

The heart of the profile for potential hires is always our core values. Any person hoping to fill any job, from caretaker to comptroller, must have integrity, character, a servant attitude, etc. Beyond those main criteria, though, we also consider upfront the other qualifications needed in great detail, applying my water pressure story to determine what great looks like at a granular level. Exactly what technical or computer skills, if any, will be required? Will the person in this role have to be a fast typist or comfortable talking to the public (you can love people and still be shy, and not every job needs a gregarious worker)?

The new Product Specialist position was so important to me and to the future of our business – actually, to the future of the industry – that I went to great lengths to make sure we'd considered what great looked like from every angle. By the time we were ready to hire the first class of Product Specialists, I felt that the role as defined did not just rely on our core values, it was their purest embodiment. Jacob, as I've pointed out, had every one of the necessary qualifications in my opinion. He met our core values and, along with his fellow Product Specialists, represented the future of our business.

While demonstrating our core values, a Jacob would give Internet-savvy consumers who didn't like the old sales model a new way to shop (those who were more comfortable working with a traditional salesperson would still have that option). Whatever minute detail a customer needed to know about a product, Jacob would have it or speedily get it. He would be able to tell them what was available at what price, obtain the product quickly, and demonstrate it without negotiating or trying to sell. The training for this position was much more stringent than any we'd previously provided.

The concept seemed solid. Jacob told me that in his early days with the company some buyers instantly relaxed when he explained that he wasn't making a commission or trying to sell them anything.

"Sometimes I would just lay it out for people and say, 'I don't want you to feel pressured. I'm not a commission-based salesman. I'm here to serve you. You can purchase if you want to, but it's not going to affect my pay in any way," Jacob said. "Some people were instantly like, 'Okay, this guy just wants to do right by me,' and they looked relieved."

If people didn't want to come to our location for a car, Jacob would bring the vehicle to them. And if they needed help, it didn't matter whether or not they were his customers. He simply acted as their advocate.

Jacob, you'll recall, turned down our first offer for a commission-based sales job. He preferred the new Product Specialist position because it would allow him to answer yes to the Four Fundamentals of Employee Engagement (not that he knew that term) and because it looked to him like a good reflection of core values that he admired.

"So the salary, you could say, was the security for me," Jacob said later about accepting the job. "But the real appeal was the idea that you could be a customer advocate without having to worry about making a sale to put food on the table. So you could put more focus on helping the customer. And then there was a ladder, a clear ladder to climb for a career with the company. It was no longer just a nine-to-five job but a long-term position laid out before me. *Oh, there's somewhere to go with this, it's a stepping stone.*"

Jacob felt that this would be important work, allowing him to help people He would **matter, be heard, grow,** and be **compensated fairly**. And as you can see from his thoughts above, the ways that he wanted to serve the customer aligned perfectly with our core values. I couldn't have been happier with the new position and our new hire.

We had done so much right as an organization, how could our prized program, the embodiment of our core values, be going wrong? Well, for starters, I broke one of the important rules of leadership – get buy-in from everyone. The GMs bought in, but their belief and engagement did not cascade down to the next level.

In the coming chapters, I'll analyze more of what we did right in changing our culture, why the new program still failed initially, and the strategies we used to correct course. Every organization attempting to grow or improve faces missteps similar to ours, so whether you work at a tiny store or run a sizeable company, I hope that you will draw practical lessons from our experience.

THE TAKEAWAYS

- An enormous number of problems at organizations arise because team members don't know *what great looks like.* When the direction is not clear, we do what *we think* is important.
- You get what you settle for if you don't know what you want.
- Strong leaders take the time to decide and write down what they want, what *great* looks like, and then communicate it effectively. This starts with identifying core values.
- Core values must emerge organically from what *you* want as an organization, what great looks like for *your* team and *your* clients. No 2 sets should be exactly the same.
- Core values will help you recruit, hire, fire, train, strategize, manage, advertise, etc. Used properly, they become embedded in the organization's DNA.
- Core values differentiate your organization, provide competitive advantage, and aid in the transition from being talent-driven to being process-driven.
- By attracting like-minded people, core values result in less turnover, more satisfied productive team members, and smoother management.
- Apart from core values, managers should also decide *what great looks like* on a granular level before advertising openings. Exactly what skills and qualities will the ideal candidate have?

EXERCISE: ESTABLISHING CORE VALUES

I once again recommend that you read the book *Traction: Get a Grip on Your Business* as you begin work on core values. The following exercise to define core values relies on the steps that author Gino Wickman outlines there.

1. Set aside a day and gather your senior managers for a discussion of core values.
2. Ask each leader to identify three stellar team members within the organization. These should be workers who, if you could clone them, would allow you to dominate your industry. Put all of the names up on a board or screen. Eliminate overlap.
3. Next have your managers name the characteristics that prompted them to choose their three people. Write these traits on the board or screen and, again, eliminate overlap. (This is also an exercise I use to review actual real-time influences. If I'm engaging with an employee and think there could be a relationship issue, I might ask the team member to name three people who we could dominate the industry with if they could be cloned. If the team member's supervisor is not on the list, he or she is probably not listening and leading the way Amanda taught me to).
4. Of these characteristics, discuss with your managers the traits that are most important to your organization, the ones you value most as people and professionals, the ones most critical to reaching organizational goals.
5. Narrow your list down until you have three to six core values (fewer than three is probably too slim and not very useful; more than half a dozen becomes unwieldy for most organizations, and dilutes focus). Be honest in choosing – no sugar-coating. Make sure that everyone in the room has a voice and is listened to. To succeed, the process must be collaborative.
6. Once you have established core values, incorporate them into your recruiting, hiring, training, performance reviews, decision making, strategic planning, etc. If the effort is undertaken with sincerity, your core values should become an integral part of the organization, present in its every fiber.

CHAPTER 4

Developing World-Class Training

Shifting the focus from talent to process transforms organizational culture

Some years ago, a trusted vendor who operated a magazine in which we advertised came to me with a question. "John, is it my job to send customers to you or to sell them after they get to you?" he asked.

I told him that his only job was to bring us customers – the rest was up to our team.

"Well then," he said, "Would you mind taking a minute to listen to a few of the recorded calls coming in to one of your stores?"

The store in question wanted to fire this vendor and stop advertising in his publication because the ads weren't delivering. The problem was that the vendor actually drove more leads to this store than to any other in the organization. From his perspective, he was doing his job, but the ball got dropped when potential customers called our location.

I immediately agreed to listen to some calls, as he suggested. Thank goodness I did. When we sat down to listen to calls at that location what I heard, frankly, was horrifying. Incoming sales calls are a chance to build lifelong relationships. They're a source of profit and equally important, a reflection of who we are, so I take them very seriously. Some of the calls I listened to were answered well, but many were sloppy, unfocused, and unprofessional.

Our team members' poor phone performance was especially painful because I pride myself on the kind of training that should have prevented it. I used to be the guy who trained all of the new hires coming into our company. This was one of the fundamentals that I built my career on, so falling short in this area was acutely embarrassing.

Naturally, the next day I headed to that store first thing to personally train all of our salespeople on phone etiquette and procedures. Meticulously, I went through my whole presentation, the same training I'd done for years. At the end of it, I cold-called various businesses similar to ours to demonstrate for our team members how well or how poorly they were doing.

Next, I called some people within our own organization, including my longtime manager Ken, to see how they handled calls. As expected, Ken was articulate and professional. He did a great job, no question about it, but he did not answer the call exactly as I would have. What I was teaching team members that day was a little different from what he was teaching the employees at his store. Other managers were no doubt injecting their own preferences and styles into the mix too.

I realized that as our organization grew, we pulled in people at various levels who had trained at companies all over the country. Their approaches were often effective and often similar, but never quite the same. This meant that an employee working under multiple supervisors might be doing a good job one day and, without changing a thing, a poor job the next. What made one supervisor happy could annoy another to no end.

The sales staff handling incoming calls did not know what *great* looked like, or rather, they had multiple, varying pictures of *great* to contend with. This was a recipe for confusion and inconsistency that had to be fixed.

EXPERIENCE MAPPING

We immediately went back to the drawing board. I huddled in a room with six or seven of our top leaders to optimize our process for answering calls. I had been through the Disney Institute's professional development course and used a version of Disney's experience mapping technique as our organizing principle. This terrific tool can help any organization diagram any task or process into clear chronological steps.

To map a process this way, place the task at hand in the center of a wheel – in our case, this task was *answering inbound phone calls.* The first step in the process is then listed in a circle extending from the first spoke, in the twelve o'clock position – in our case, *greet the customer.* Moving clockwise, the second step is listed in a circle attached to the second spoke, around one o'clock. For us, this was *ask the customer two questions about the vehicle they want, to assure them that we are there to serve them.* Mapping continues around the wheel, one spoke for each step, until the task is complete [see diagram below].

These wheels are simple, clear representations that break a process down into easily digestible parts for both management and team members. They can contain as many or as few spokes as needed, depending on the complexity or duration of the task, and if necessary, each step can be broken down with its own wheel. For instance, if I wanted to map step one of my sales process, *greet the customer,* in detail, I would move it to the center of a new wheel and make the first step, at twelve o'clock, *Clear your mind of all other activities.* Step two, at one o'clock, might be *Make sure you communicate clearly and with a smile on your face that can be felt through the tone of your voice,* etc. [see diagram below].

My leadership team and I discussed the best ways to handle incoming leads, from greeting customers to discussing pricing to, hopefully, ending a call with a scheduled appointment. Everyone's approach was a little bit different, but overall, they were pretty similar. Before long, we'd settled our debates and together, mapped what we thought was a terrific phone process. It was the first time we'd mapped a process on a wheel this way, but the steps themselves were not much different from those in the first script I'd been given twenty-five years ago.

We brought in some of our sales managers and salespeople to see what they thought. A lot of the response was positive, and then one of the younger salespeople in the room tentatively raised a hand.

"Excuse me, Mr. Hiester?" he said.

I pointed his way and said, "Yes sir."

"Well, the thing is, people don't ask these kinds of questions anymore."

I asked what he meant, looking, I'm sure, as confused as I felt.

"With the Internet now, everybody already knows you have a good price," he said. "That's why they're calling you. They've done all their research online. The customers' problem is the lowest priced car that they called about is already sold when they arrive, or it was misrepresented, so they're going to the next dealership on the list."

The only things that customers who call want to know now, this young man said, is: *Do you have the car I want?* and *Is it as it was represented online?*

When I was the age of this millennial salesperson, incoming calls were all about price. Everyone wanted the best one, and people found a great deal by calling around. Technology had changed the industry, though, and I saw immediately that this young man was right. The phone protocol that we'd worked so hard to outline was basically a cookie-cutter training script that any company might use, one that was decades out of date and answered questions that people no longer asked.

We wadded up our first experience map to start over, this time focusing on the dynamics that our frontline workers answering calls were actually encountering. We began the new process with "ask two confirming questions." Once we had that info, we would put the customer on hold to quickly check on the vehicle's availability and to pull the keys if it was in stock. The next step grew directly from our millennial team member's observation that the customer's biggest problem in the Internet age was not finding a good price but that the right vehicle with the right price disappeared before they got to the store. To address this, we would offer to place the vehicle on hold, so that customers could come take a look at it – something I'd never seen another business in our industry do.

This was a game-changer because every other store we knew of said, "Well, it's first come, first served." We, on the other hand, would now serve customers in the way that they wanted, a way that made sense in the digital age. "Yes, we have that exact vehicle. Would you like me to place it on hold for you, so that you may come take a look at it?" At that point, customers would typically respond, "Wow, you do that?" What's more, if customers couldn't make an appointment that day, we would offer to bring the vehicle to them. This was another bold move, a service our competitors didn't offer. The reason most dealerships didn't offer this was that commissioned sales people did not want to leave the store and miss another opportunity. Hiring Jacob and our other Product Specialists would remove this barrier because they were salaried and more than happy to take a road trip to demonstrate products.

DEVELOPING WRITTEN REPEATABLE PROCESS

Change is never easy, and our phone training was no exception. After we went through the involved process I just described, we got buy-in from everyone in the organization and worked on our training techniques. Finally, we had a phone protocol that was consistent and measurable. This is key because until you know what great looks like, you cannot hold people accountable to it.

Soon after, unfortunately, our manufacturers began insisting that we meet their phone training requirements to qualify for various incentives. The corporate trainers came out and looked at our process. No, they said, we want you to move to this other basic system that has worked for twenty years.

And then they saw our success rate.

Tracking indicated that our conversion rate (the number of callers who become customers) was almost 12 percent higher than theirs. Suddenly, instead of insisting on their script, one of the guys that the manufacturer recommended we contract with wanted to know if he could steal ours.

The success of our new phone protocols spurred us to reexamine every part of our business, all of our processes and training, to see how we could better serve our customers and to find places where our best practices weren't keeping up with a changing marketplace. Ultimately, our new phone process wasn't about writing an innovative script so much as it was creating a new business model, one that emphasized service and had a systematic approach that we could follow step by step for consistency among all of our brands.

This approach in part led to our core values initiative, and it was the first step toward developing our Product Specialist position. I can draw a direct line from our development of a new phone process and thinking about Internet-driven changes in consumer behavior to hiring Jacob, a consumer advocate who was college-educated, career-minded, highly knowledgeable about products, and not paid by commission. I can draw another line from that phone experience to the Hiester Valet app we custom-developed with a software company to allow customers to schedule pickups and drop-offs of their vehicles, order work, get video confirmation of needed repairs, and pay – all with a few taps on their cell phones.

I could list many more changes that this phone training led to but the overarching cultural change is one I have mentioned briefly – the switch from being a talent-driven organization to being a process-driven one. My manager is a very talented guy with many talented people working for him. His team members often achieved good results before we revamped our phone training, but they achieved better results afterwards. Now *everyone* who answers incoming calls at the organization does so in a consistent manner that guarantees a high level of service and aligns with our core values.

Employees who switch locations or get a new manager within the organization now know with certainty that they will be following the same process. They know exactly what *great* looks like and having clear protocols written down is critical to maintaining that standard.

The vast majority of your team members want to do good, I have argued, and when they don't seem to be pulling their weight, it's usually because you have not adequately conveyed what *great* looks like. Once I realized that I'd been guilty of this managerial sin with our phone protocols and defined *great* there, I worked with my leadership team to examine all sorts of processes within the organization in order to set standards and detail procedures.

The process wheel that helps staff answer incoming sales calls was only the first of dozens we developed. Pretty much every position in the organization now has at least one and often several of these wheels.

I caution you here. People tend to think that this strategy is micromanaging. I would argue that when employees know exactly what is expected of them and how they will be measured, they know how to please, and it frees them up. Suddenly, they can devote their brain power to other challenges within your organization because they aren't spending time guessing what you want them to accomplish.

The Product Specialist position that Jacob filled, for example, includes around half a dozen process wheels. The first of them details the big steps that the overall job requires. The next wheel breaks down the first step in that process.

I believe experience mapping is very beneficial because the process wheel it produces creates a quick clear visual that's easy to reference. You can imagine, for instance, new employees following along on our phone process wheel during training sessions and then keeping it on their desk afterwards, during the first weeks of live calls to make sure they are following each step correctly.

Not everything will fit on a wheel, however. We also developed detailed "process manuals" for every position, expanded our job descriptions, and built measurables into our written materials. Organizations should have these three elements for every job in order to build Written Repeatable Process and shift from a focus on talent (the lone-wolf model) to a focus on process (the team model):

- **Job description**
- **3-5 measurables**
- **Process manual**

ELEMENT ONE: JOB DESCRIPTION

Most organizations have job descriptions of some sort, but they often lack important components. We always start with a brief summary upfront that boils the position down to its essentials in a sentence or two. Without this, it's easy for the true purpose of the job to get lost in a barrage of information. In other words, a summary prevents employees from missing the forest for the trees. The summary that Jacob encountered when he became a Product Specialist was:

Product Specialists are to be well informed about all vehicles, thus being able to show those vehicles to potential customers. Their main focus is to ensure that the customer is completely satisfied with their entire experience at John Hiester Automotive.

Conveying the individual's *why* and how it contributes to the organizational *why* is critical in getting team members to answer *yes* to the first and most important of the Four Fundamentals of Employee Engagement: *Do I matter / bring value?* It's key to engagement and performance – and it makes managers' lives a heck of a lot easier. Job descriptions vary widely in length and content, but in addition to conveying purpose, they should also generally include concrete standards for individuals and their work, and a list of daily tasks and responsibilities. A pay scale should be included and, if possible, linked to training and advancement.

Our Product Specialist job description, for instance, lists seven distinct levels, each with its own training regimen, product presentation requirements, and pay grade. Detailing in writing a concrete path for advancement provides employees with clear standards and expectations, as well as goals to aim for. The beauty of this is that when employees have a ladder to look at, with levels of achievement and pay, they tend to focus on reaching their next level, as opposed to looking at where there next outside opportunity is going to come from.

By the time we developed the Product Specialist position, our shift to being a process-driven organization was advanced, and Written Repeatable Process was at the heart of the operation. Linking a pay scale to a path upward, one tied to training, education, certifications, or other milestones, allows employees to answer *yes* to two more of our Four Fundamentals of Employee Engagement: *Am I growing / developing?* and *Am I fairly compensated?*

A job description, to review, should include:

- **Job Summary**, 1-2 sentences upfront defining the purpose of the position, its *why*
- **Standards** for the individual, the work, the organization
- **Daily tasks** outlined in a thorough list, descriptions
- **Pay scale**, tied to an advancement path (certifications, education, experience, etc.)

ELEMENT TWO: THE 3-5 MEASURABLES

The measurables outlined in your process manual must be concrete, meaning they should include at least some numbers. They should also be fruit-bearing. That might suggest a direct tie to sales, profits, production volume, etc. but not necessarily. The key measure for Jacob's position as a Product Specialist, for instance, is the number of product demonstrations completed per week. That isn't directly tied to profits, but since we know from experience just how many product demonstrations will ultimately result in a sale, it is a "fruit-bearing" metric. Three to five key measurables provide a good picture of employee performance.

ELEMENT THREE: THE PROCESS MANUAL

A process manual is larger and more thorough. It includes the job description and concrete measurables, and it details the range of processes that someone in a particular position must engage in. Not only should there be no doubt about what *great* looks like once a team member has read the appropriate process manual, he or she should have concrete expectations for daily performance and clear routes for moving up the ranks, getting questions answered, resolving conflicts, etc.

Like our job descriptions, our process manuals start with our *why*, in this case, the organization's overarching purpose: our mission statement, core values, and core focus. Next, we include the organizational structure, a chart outlining hierarchy and responsibilities and how various departments relate to each other. This shows team members how they're contributing to the overall organization and where they fit in the chain of command.

After printing the job description in each position's process manual, we get into the nitty-gritty of every process that someone doing this job will have to engage in, demonstrated through process wheels / experience mapping, descriptions, checklists, etc. As I noted earlier, the process manual for our Product Specialists includes around half a dozen process wheels, from *meet and greet* to *demo drive* to *car rating*, breaking the job down for trainees and providing standards against which employees can be measured.

A good process manual for each position then should include the following:

- **Purpose / *why*,** conveyed through mission statement, core values, core focus, etc.
- **Organizational chart,** showing hierarchy, direct reports, etc.
- **Job description** (see bullets above)
- **All processes** this job entails, including experience maps / process wheels (or flow charts, other tools), descriptions, checklists, etc.
- **Measurables,** 3-5 fruit-bearing metrics that include numbers
- **Programs / policies** that people in this position must know

- **Support materials**, necessary forms, paperwork, etc.
- **Written and digital versions**, substantially the same, though links to training videos, pertinent information sources, etc. are obviously more accessible in digital form

MORE EFFECTIVE MANAGEMENT

If you're feeling overwhelmed about now, don't panic. Yes, this sort of culture change can seem daunting depending on your starting point, but I want to emphasize two things here. First, the creation of Written Repeatable Process doesn't happen overnight. We did not develop all our process wheels, manuals, and job descriptions in a single month. You can do this gradually and systematically, position by position, and it will grow easier each time as you become a more process-oriented organization. Recently, we have assigned our management team the task of creating and documenting three processes per manager within each of their departments, so that we can update or draw new maps for our current employees.

The second thing I want to emphasize is that your investment in developing Written Repeatable Process will pay massive dividends later in easier, more effective management. The difference between managing our team before we focused on Written Repeatable Process and after was night and day. Employees had a much clearer picture of expectations, tasks, and responsibilities. They had a go-to resource in both written and digital formats detailing exactly what they had to do, how it would be measured, the ways they could move forward, and how they would be compensated.

Our team members weren't just better trained, they knew what *great* looked like and were much more likely to answer *yes* to the Four Fundamentals of Employee Engagement. Eliminating guesswork for team members frees them. And managers overseeing employees with better training, motivation, knowledge, and resources could spend less time explaining, correcting, and yelling. They could focus on the big picture. They could stop supervising and begin leading.

Our whole organization ran better and our service became consistent regardless of manager, location, or day of the week. The "Written" part of Written Repeatable Process is key for the consistency that any organization wants in employee performance. A process that is explained rather than written out, or one that's written partially or unclearly, will change and evolve through no fault of employees. Over time, instead of *a* repeatable process, you have twenty ad hoc processes offering various levels of quality and service.

When I think about this in terms of my family's experiences, I recall that both of my daughters worked for Chik-Fil-A when they were in school. Ashley became a team leader there. Before she got that promotion, she was required to watch twelve hours of videos detailing the processes that she would be accountable for, followed by quizzes that required a passing grade in order for her to advance. Corporate leaders understood that the more detailed the process manual was, even at the entry level, the more consistent the products / service the company could offer to all customers. I believe, based on my experience, that Chik-Fil-A is one of the best at this in its industry.

I often tell leaders to think about Written Repeatable Process in terms of the old game of "telephone," which you might have played as a kid. It begins with somebody whispering a short phrase to someone, who then whispers it to the next person, who whispers it to the next, and so on. It doesn't take long before *carefully plan your attack* becomes *murder all the cats*. If you leave room for interpretation, employees will put their own spin on things. Instructions will get altered, procedures will morph. For the purposes of this chapter, maybe we should add a phrase to the precept I discussed in Chapter 3: if you don't know what you want *and communicate it well*, you'll settle for what you get.

Once you know what you want, Written Repeatable Process is the surest way to communicate and achieve it. Document as much of every process as you can *in writing*. A process can still be changed, of course, but once it's embedded in process manuals and job descriptions and tied to measurables, changing it takes a lot more work – new analysis, the collaboration of team leaders, feedback from the frontline, amendments to the process manual, etc. It's more likely that only good ideas producing meaningful change will survive when it's as tough to change established best practices as it is to pass a bill in Congress.

Creating Written Repeatable Process and changing organizational culture can be arduous, but rather than being daunted, think of such efforts as an opportunities to optimize positions and procedures, unleashing your team's talent. It took time and effort to develop our new phone process. Was it frustrating to realize we'd spent hours coming up with a dated phone script that then had to be scrapped? Absolutely. Did creating the new experience maps, process manuals and other materials, and retraining staff require effort? Sure. But at the end of the day, we had a phone process that we still think is one of the best in the industry. We began turning more callers into customers, which boosted our bottom line.

More important, we emerged with a much better understanding of our customers and how they wanted to shop in the digital age. We became better attuned to our market and gained an edge over the competition. We became better servants.

What processes within your organization might be outdated or inconsistent or not serving your customers in the ways that they want today? Taking the time to explore procedures as a team, with feedback from those on the frontline, will almost certainly result in better ones. In addition to making management easier, developing Written Repeatable Process will improve your organization in all sorts of unforeseen ways. We certainly had no idea when we set out to write a consistent phone script that the effort would lead to our Hiester Valet app, a new Product Specialist position, and, ultimately, a new business model.

BUILD IN ACCOUNTABILITY

By the time we hired Jacob, as I noted earlier, our journey to develop Written Repeatable Process was far along, so why was one of his eight criticisms of the Product Specialist program about training? The training, you'll recall, was good at first, Jacob said – and then nothing.

The first two weeks of training for Product Specialists occurred off-site, at the location where I keep my office. This was my pet program, living under my watchful eye, and the initial training there was excellent. Once the Product Specialists, who were considered trainees for their first ninety days, moved off-site to work in other locations, however, their managers did not follow through. Solid initial training and thorough Written Repeatable Process will slide if you don't build accountability into the system.

I took Jacob's criticism to heart in the spirit of *fix me first*, and as an organization, we began to formalize all training. From shortly after my meeting with Jacob, when he described a training deficit, we began requiring that managers turn in monthly training schedules. We no longer simply specified that a department had to do this or that training. From then on, managers had to list:

- **Who is doing the training**
- **The topic to be covered**
- **When the training is scheduled**
- **Confirmation the training occurred**

Without this kind of accountability, the effort put into even the best Written Repeatable Process will be undermined, if not wasted. If more than one person is responsible, we firmly believe, no one is responsible.

The accountability we built into training is another example of deciding what you want *and communicating it well*, and actually stems from our core value of *loves people*. It's hard to blame someone for failing to engage training if it's unclear exactly who will be doing what training and when. Once a schedule is established, leaders must then answer for any shortfalls. Love of people is not simply about hugs and kind words. It also means that you have to love someone enough to hold him or her accountable.

I've only touched on accountability here as it relates to training, but it is so important to effective management, I will devote the next chapter to this topic, exploring measurables, success checkpoints, and the practicalities of showing your team what *great* looks like.

THE TAKEAWAYS

- Experience mapping can turn a complicated process into a clear, easily digestible diagram that helps team members provide consistent quality and service.
- To build Written Repeatable Process, organizations should have the following for every position:
  o Job Description
  o 3-5 Measurables
  o Process manual
- The purpose, or *why*, of a job should be conveyed prominently in all job descriptions and emphasized as part of all training and Written Repeatable Process.
- A job description should include:
  o Job Summary
  o Standards
  o Daily Tasks
  o Pay Scale
- The process manual for every position should include:
  o Purpose / *why*, conveyed through mission statement, core values, core focus, etc.
  o Organizational Chart, showing hierarchy, direct reports, etc.
  o Job description
  o All Processes this job entails, including experience maps, flow charts, etc.
  o 3-5 measurables, fruit-bearing metrics that include numbers
  o Programs / policies that people in this position must know
  o Support materials, necessary forms, paperwork, etc.
  o Written and digital versions
- Our Written Repeatable Process began with the need to adjust one procedure that at first, we didn't even know was lacking. I advise choosing one area where you feel deficient and start building Written Repeatable Process there.
- Build accountability into your training (and everything): **If more than one person is responsible, no one is responsible.**

- Training schedules are a must for accountability. Managers should systematically report:
  o Who is doing the training
  o The topic to be covered
  o When the training is scheduled
  o Confirmation the training occurred

EXERCISE: EXPERIENCE MAPPING

Experience mapping is an invaluable tool for thinking about and improving the processes vital to your organization, as well as for training team members to perform them consistently. The same basic strategy can take a variety of forms – timelines, flow charts, wheels, etc. In this exercise, I'll walk you through the creation of our preferred tool, a process wheel like those used by the Disney Institute. This is a simple, clear way to visually represent a process. It can include as many or as few steps as necessary, so it works well whether the process is *eating soup* or *changing nuclear fuel rods*. Each step in the wheel can become its own wheel, too, so the process can be examined on as macro or micro a level as you want.

1. Choose a position within the organization and think about the overall process it involves (as we did with our phone sales staff example in this chapter).
2. Place the overall task or job in a circle that will become the center of a wheel (in our example, "answering calls").
3. Draw a line or spoke vertically from the first circle and attach a circle to it, in the twelve o'clock position. List the first step in the process in this circle (in our example, "greet the customer").
4. Moving clockwise, draw another spoke to the right of the first and attach a circle to it in the one o'clock position. Write the second step in this circle (for us, "ask about the vehicle in question").
5. Continue clockwise around the wheel, adding one spoke for each step until the process is complete [see diagram below].
6. Get feedback from leaders and frontline workers involved in the process. What steps in the overall process are missing or weak? Can any steps be combined or improved? Should any be eliminated? Think of your customers' journey around this wheel. Is every step addressing their needs, lifestyles, and preferences

in the digital age? How can you better serve them by changing your process?

7. When your team has a wheel that it's happy with, consider which steps warrant breaking out for their own process wheels – as we did with "meet and greet" and other steps in our phone process. Place the next step you want to focus on in its own wheel and repeat this process.

CHAPTER 5
What Does Great Look Like?

Building solid metrics begins with defining what "great work" means

Charles M. Schwab, who began his career as an engineer in Andrew Carnegie's steelworks and went on to become the first president of U.S. Steel, faced a problem in the early 1900s. One of the company's mills was not producing as much as it should have. The manager, a capable man in Schwab's eyes, said he'd tried everything but couldn't seem to boost production. I can imagine how that meeting went – no doubt, there even thoughts of closing the plant.

About a week later, Schwab visited the plant to try and analyze the situation. I imagine he saw that the company had great people at a facility capable of accomplishing its expectations, but they were not failing. The mill had three shifts each day. As the day shift was getting off, Mr. Schwab approached a foreman and asked how many heats his shift had made.

"Six," the man replied.

Without uttering another word, Schwab chalked a giant 6 on the floor and left.

When the night shift started, workers saw the 6 and asked what it meant. The day-shift workers explained that the big boss had been in and asked how many heats they'd done. Six, they had told him, and without a word, he'd written the number there in chalk.

The night shift made sure that when they left, they erased the 6 to chalk a 7 – the number of heats they had done. Seeing that they'd been bested by the night shift, the day shift upped their game and by the time they punched out, were able to chalk a big 10 in place of the 7.

Soon, this underperforming mill became the company's best producer.

The lesson I draw from this story is one I've mentioned briefly but will focus on here, since it's at the core of this book. Most people want to do good. They want to please and excel and to turn out great work, but they don't know what *great* looks like. Leaders usually have some big-picture idea of how *great* looks – *we want to sell 40,000 widgets next quarter,* or *we should bill 20 percent more than last year* – but they do not translate the organization's vision of *great* into terms that make sense for an individual team member's role and daily work.

To share one of my favorite measurement metaphors, leaders are focused on the fruit they'll harvest and not the elements that go into producing it – the seeds, soil, water, etc.

Schwab's company had been making the same mistake, relying on the amount of steel sold as its definition of *great*. The problem is that many elements factor into the amount of steel sold. A wide variety of workers contribute in all sorts of ways, doing all sorts of jobs, and so, focusing on that final result, *the fruit,* means that no one actually gets held responsible for anything. Is the company falling short on steel sales because of inefficiencies in its iron mining operations or at the blast furnaces or in casting? Is the administration bloated or is the sales staff aiming too low?

Schwab took things down to a more basic level when he chalked that "6" on the floor. What produces the fruit, and what sort of metric will be meaningful to *these* workers doing *this* job? What does *great* look like for them? Conveying *great* in such vague terms as "we need to sell more steel" creates a vacuum in which employees will do what they think you want. A gap inevitably rises then between leaders' goals and workers' performance. Indicating that 6 heats per shift is good and 10 is great, on the other hand, leaves no room for guesswork.

Schwab was probably tempted to blame the workers for low production, and maybe his manager already had, but clearly the mill's employees were capable of the work and wanted to excel. Of course they did. If we vet our employees correctly and they're right for the job when we hire them, if they start out doing well and then fail later, it's almost never their fault. That failure usually arises because the boss has not broken big goals down into clear measurables that meaningfully gauge the things producing the fruit.

If the right metrics are in place, team members are either hitting them or not. If they are not, then they should know that immediately, and it's the boss's job to figure out why and coach them up to speed. The poor performance so often blamed on laziness, inattention, or incompetence usually indicates poor metrics, or a failure to communicate and monitor good ones.

When organizations take the time to devise, communicate, and monitor the right metrics, however, the results can be astonishing, as they were for Schwab once he chalked that "6" on the mill floor. Good metrics engage employees, stoking their motivation and resourcefulness. Defining *great* intelligently is not about binding team members or pinning them down, although this misguided approach is common. Good metrics liberate employees and turn them into problem solvers. *We need to hit 7 heats today, come hell or high water. Let's find a way to do it.* Good measurables prevent surprises for both team members and leaders, clarify expectations, and build team dynamics while helping workers answer *yes* to the Four Fundamentals of Employee Engagement.

FIND YOUR SIX

Our approach to metrics began to change as we became a more process-driven organization, the evolution I described in the last chapter. When talent is your driver, the focus remains squarely on the result, those final sales numbers for the month, quarter, year – or the number of customers served, widgets sold, etc. This is your fruit, just as the amount of steel sold was Schwab's.

Shifting your focus to process, however, leads inevitably to new thinking on metrics. If we're investing time and energy in defining our processes and betting our success on their effectiveness and consistency, you begin to think, hadn't we better build measures into them? Shifting to a process-driven approach automatically gets you thinking about and measuring the things that produce the fruit rather than just the fruit itself. Sales numbers are easy to measure. Finding the right metrics for the right steps in a complex process is not. Schwab and his manager had both tried for some time to fix the company's troubled mill before Schwab chalked that magic 6 on the floor.

Jacob's story also offers a prime example of the difficulty and effectiveness of intelligent, process-based metrics. I had never worked so hard on measurement or thought so deeply about it as when we created the Product Specialist position. I'm still proud of the measurables we built into that job, and yet every one of the eight reasons that Jacob gave for leaving related in some way to how he was measured. Getting measurables right, I realized after my meeting with him, was critical not only to retaining a valued employee, but also to ensuring the survival of our evolving business model.

The Product Specialist role that Jacob was hired to fill, you'll recall, stemmed partly from our attempt to address the objections that career-minded college-educated millennials had to working in our industry:

- **The stigma of being a car salesperson**
- **The uncertainty of commission-based pay**
- **Resistance to one-on-one negotiations**
- **Long hours**

We addressed those objections through development of the new position, but also through new metrics, which were as important as the job itself. If we were to attract career-minded college-educated millennials, they would have to work in roles that did not involve selling and negotiating, and which weren't based on commission. I have already described how the Product Specialist role – more like a Mac Genius at an Apple Store than a traditional salesperson – met these requirements. We were excited about the idea of the new position, but it forced the question: how do we measure and pay these people? What should our "6" be?

Like many sales-based organizations, we knew how to measure and pay salespeople – according to how much they sold. And we knew exactly how many sales we needed in order to pay everyone, keep the lights on, and earn a profit. Product Specialists like Jacob, however, would not engage in sales – that was the whole point.

It seemed a dilemma at first, but Product Specialists would do presentations – this was the heart of the job – and we knew from internal data that four presentations almost always resulted in one sale. The number could vary depending on a particular day, salesperson, etc., but we're careful about tracking the numbers, and that average was solid.

Presentations are not sales but because we knew how many sales they would produce, we could work backwards from the necessary number of sales to create a pay scale and measurement regimen that made sense for both the Product Specialists and the organization. We figured out that for a Product Specialist at Level 1 or Level 2, six presentations a week would be what *great* looked like (don't feel that you must work a six into your metrics; the fact that our number here mirrors Carnegie's is pure coincidence). Given their pay grade, we needed each Product Specialist at those levels to do around twenty-six presentations per month because that would produce 6.5 monthly sales, enough to pay for the program.

If Product Specialists were hitting their six presentations per week and finished several specified trainings, after 180 days, they could move up to Level 3. That advancement came with a pay bump, and then *great* became eight presentations per week. The higher target would pay for their higher salary, and made sense anyway, since they would be more experienced, better trained, and more comfortable with the products by then.

In all, we carved out seven levels for Product Specialists, as I've noted, each with a designated pay rate and specific targets for trainings, education, number of presentations required, etc. These metrics made sense for the organization and for the individual. I have explained how they addressed college-educated millennials' objections to our industry, but – and this is critical – I knew that our new measurables would have been meaningless if we didn't emphasize the *why* behind them.

Telling a team member, *Hey, we want you to do six presentations per week* is about as effective as saying, *We want to sell more steel* if you don't emphasize the purpose behind the number. This is where so many leaders, even those with terrific metrics, fall down. We had to explain to our Product Specialists in concrete terms the ways that presentations lead to sales. *Here is how and why we arrived at this exact number, and here's why your hitting it is vital to our overall mission and to the success of the organization.* Emphasizing the *why* with metrics is key to motivating employees. They are more likely to produce the numbers you want when you share how team members and their efforts fit into your larger strategy. This kind of inclusion addresses the first of our Four Fundamentals of Employee Engagement: *Do I matter / bring value?* Suddenly, employees like Jacob think, *my making six presentations this week really matters to the success of this organization. I am important.*

Good measurables should also address the last two Fundamentals: *Am I growing and developing?* and *Am I fairly compensated?* The Product Specialist position, with its seven levels spelling out training requirements, pay, and advancement for each, as well as presentation targets, did this. Jacob knew exactly how to move forward on a specific time frame tied to performance when we hired him, and he saw the pay bumps spelled out along the way. (Your system of measurables should also address the second of the Four Fundamentals, *Am I heard?* and we'll address that later, when we explore feedback).

Good, clearly communicated metrics also convey your core values to employees and customers. We created this position and its unique metrics to attract recruits with a high degree of character, integrity, and professionalism. Measuring them by the number of presentations they did, not according to sales, reinforced those qualities. Their only motivation was to be as helpful to the customer as possible and to share their expertise.

"The real appeal was the idea that you could be a customer advocate without having to worry about making a sale to put food on the table," Jacob later said of his decision to take the job. "So you could put more focus on helping the customer."

That's exactly the kind of servant attitude, love of people, and get-it-done approach we wanted in our new hires, and these core values lived in the metrics we evaluated them on. Product Specialists weren't worried about making a sale (the fruit) because they weren't measured based on sales. They were graded according to how many people they helped through product presentations, as well as on the knowledge, training, and skills they acquired as they moved through various levels.

The organization's metrics conveyed our core values to customers, as well as internally. When you stop trying to sell somebody and simply seek to serve them as well as you possibly can, trust gets built. Jacob often told customers that he didn't get paid any differently if they decided not to buy a vehicle, and this seemed to put them at ease. A relationship developed, and customers ended up buying from him because they wanted to, not only because we had the best price. Consumers who dealt with our Product Specialists appreciated the core values they exhibited and pegged them as true servants who weren't worried about selling.

Ironically, our sales rate rose once we stopped focusing on sales. I noted earlier that we built this program and its metrics on the idea that four presentations produced one sale. The ratio for Product Specialists, who weren't measured by sales, however, actually turned out to be closer to three to one. I'm sure it sounded counterintuitive, if not a little crazy, when early in this chapter I encouraged readers to focus on the things producing the fruit and not the fruit itself, but we have put our money where our mouth is, and our Product Specialist numbers prove the point. Farmers get this. They don't spend their time counting next autumn's apples, but measuring soil, fertilizers, irrigation, pickers…Focus on and measure what produces the fruit, and the fruit will come.

MAKING THE GRADE

I have written a lot here about metrics in terms of our Product Specialist position because it's a good example, but the same general lessons apply to any job, so I want to take a moment to review a few fundamentals. Leaders should develop these sorts of metrics for every position at their organization, from receptionist to salesperson to comptroller, building from the same principles, though the things measured might be quite different.

I always suggest that managers choose three to five key metrics to chart employee performance and progress. Fewer than that, and it's tough to get a complete picture. Choose too many, and both team members and managers lose focus. Gino Wickman, the author of *Traction* and the inspiration for our core values exercise in Chapter 3, advises leaders to imagine that they're stranded on a desert island and can only ask three questions remotely to see how an employee is doing. Those three queries are probably a good starting point for developing your measurables.

For every job at the organization, ask what are the three to five critical indicators? "Critical," in this case, means fruit-bearing, to continue with my metaphor, not the fruit itself. For example, our Product Specialists' demonstrations are clearly fruit-bearing (three presentations lead to one sale), but not the fruit (actual sales). Similarly, you might have a salesperson working the phones who's currently measured by quarterly or monthly dollar volume. If, however, you know that *great* works out to three sales a week and thirty calls to prospects on average result in ten appointments, and ten appointments produce three sales, then focusing on those fruit-bearing prospect calls might be a better gauge. *Great* becomes calling thirty prospects per week, which makes more sense to the salesperson, not selling $200,000 worth of product or services per quarter.

The weekly numbers you arrive at should be broken down into daily averages. I differ from some business gurus on this point, but I am a firm believer in the daily metric. Yes, anyone can have an off day, but if I should be averaging four product demonstrations per day and I only did three today, I want to go to sleep tonight thinking I have to kick butt tomorrow and get at least five done. The daily metric should not be one that a team member has go and ask a manager to calculate or report. It should be clear and obvious, info that the employee has direct access to and can impact – *I did two product demos today, cleaned eight offices, called six new leads, painted two rooms...*

We believe that if you measure your business once a year, you may have a bad year, but you probably won't have two bad years. If you measure your business once a month, you may have a bad month, but you probably won't have a bad year. If you measure your business once a week, you may have a bad week, but...Get the idea? Daily metrics help you catch and address problems quickly, and they prevent surprises. No one should have to wait until the end of the month, or even the week, to realize he or she isn't making the grade.

Though they don't necessarily have to involve dollar amounts, these key metrics should have verifiable numbers attached to them. A Product Specialist must do six demonstrations per week (a little over one a day) during his or her first 180 days. A health counselor working for an outreach program should average three home visits per day. In addition to logging eighteen hours of continuing education courses annually, a Realtor should cold-call four prospects every day and attend one community event weekly...Subjectivity is the enemy of accountability, and hard numbers leave less room for interpretation on the part of employees and managers.

It is, of course, easier to find metrics for some positions than for others. Figuring out how to measure salespeople and mechanics, who we know should produce a certain number of hours of work per day, has been relatively simple for us. But what does *great* look like for our title clerks, who complete paperwork and file owner titles and registration? As an example, title clerks must enter a note in our system every day that a title has not been received after a deal has closed and touch that deal's folder as to the action we are taking to ensure that we receive the title within the allotted time (I mean "touch" literally here – I want that folder opened and the action checked on every day). This metric is measurable and verifiable because we can review the notes, and it helps in training.

All this can start to sound complicated, but the underlying principle is simple: what is each team member's responsibility in achieving the end goal? I say "each," by the way, because while you might also need metrics to measure teams or departments, the kinds of key measurables I've been describing must be applied to the individual. Otherwise responsibility shifts. Remember, when everyone's responsible, no one's responsible.

To recap, here are some basic principles to keep in mind when developing what I call "process metrics," which are focused on fruit-bearing tasks, not the actual fruit:

- Work backwards from the big goals to find the key fruit-bearing tasks you must measure to gauge performance for each individual.
- Choose 3-5 vital metrics that will provide the best picture of performance and progress.
- Everyone needs at least one if not several *daily* measures – waiting a week to know how you're doing is too long.
- Key metrics should have verifiable numbers attached to them.
- Explain the *why* behind your metrics to all team members to get buy-in, and to show their importance in achieving larger goals.

METRICS FAIL WITHOUT FEEDBACK

Without a rigorous system for delivering feedback on metrics, even the most carefully chosen yardsticks will fail. I will describe our organization's best practices for feedback in a moment, but first, I want to come back to Jacob's story and why he decided to quit despite his hard work and the metrics we so carefully designed to measure it.

As we've seen, the primary way that we graded Jacob, and all our Product Specialists, was through the number of product demonstrations they did. The seven distinct levels I mentioned, each with a prescribed number of presentations as well as necessary trainings, certifications, etc., was the most sophisticated set of measurables and milestones we'd ever put in place. I was proud of it – I still am – and Jacob, a true servant who did not want to be a salesperson, loved the idea.

And yes, as I wrote above, all of Jacob's eight reasons for leaving related in some way to measurables. Why did our creative metrics fail?

Well, I described how vital it is to emphasize the *why* of your metrics to a worker – the purpose behind the numbers and how the measured tasks are vital to the organization's overall success. We did this with Jacob and his peers, but we failed to do the same with his manager. Our managers nodded and smiled and seemed to be on board as we rolled out the Product Specialist program, but they didn't quite grasp all that we were trying to accomplish with this new job.

The miscommunication here, which I take responsibility for, was directly related to metrics. Jacob's manager thought, okay, this guy is not actually selling vehicles, that's not how he's being paid, so what does it matter if I have him running errands and fueling up cars?

Well, it obviously mattered to Jacob. This was not how the job had been presented to him, the contradiction at the heart of his eight objections. Nothing wrong with being a sales assistant, but that was not what he was hired to do. The manager didn't care that while Jacob was off running errands, he was missing out on chances to make the presentations we measured him on, though this obviously bothered Jacob. The manager understood the value of a sale (the fruit) because that was familiar, but not the value of the fruit-bearing presentations that led to sales.

The Product Specialists' presentations were also, as I have explained, part of a new, more service-oriented business model tailored to the way consumers shop in the digital age. Jacob's position, his presentations, his metrics were vital to the future success of the organization. His manager wasn't being malicious or lazy, he simply didn't understand the importance of a Jacob. He didn't grasp the *why* partly because I did not adequately explain how a Jacob fit into the big picture.

As I have said, changing culture is not easy. Humans, especially humans responsible for other humans, like the familiar, the known quantity. In addition to missing the point of Jacob's job, which told Jacob that he did not matter (eliciting a *no* on the First Fundamental of Employee Engagement), his manager tracked Product Specialists' "sales" up on the board anyway – the number of vehicles sold as a result of their presentations.

"If we are not salespeople and we're not supposed to be selling, then why are you tracking our sales?" Jacob asked when we sat down to review his reasons for leaving. "Doesn't that go against your core values of character and integrity, and professionalism?"

I did not have a good answer. He was right. We had a good metric – product presentations – but it was being undercut by a manager who didn't understand its *why* and instead fell back on a more comfortable measure, one that disengaged these new employees and undermined the whole purpose of the program.

I was grateful I had the opportunity to learn all of this from Jacob's perspective while he still worked for us, but his manager should have been onto these issues much earlier. If there is a problem with metrics and someone isn't making the grade, for any reason, this should come to light in regularly scheduled feedback sessions.

At our organization, every department has a weekly vision meeting. This is a chance to solve problems and set priorities. It gives the whole group a chance to bring up issues and to find clarity and focus for the coming week. We also have one-on-one quarterly evaluations in which team members sit down with their managers to discuss performance, progress, and goals. And there's the daily huddle. We want our managers to look in the eyes of each team member every day, and make sure that player is ready to step onto the field.

Metrics are discussed individually on a daily basis. Leaders should not only be cheering good work and questioning deficits in the daily huddles but also practicing active listening and building trust. If Jacob's manager had been listening the way that we want our leaders to, he should have understood much sooner that he had an employee who was becoming disengaged. He should have seen that this team member was confused by our metrics. If he truly had a fix-me-first attitude, he would have realized that this confusion was our fault for telling Product Specialists that they weren't salespeople and then measuring their sales.

Within the context of a strong feedback system, metrics aren't just about employee performance. An open discussion of the reasons for a shortfall can also reveal management mistakes, bottlenecks, system flaws, core values infractions, or a process out of whack. Feedback should be a two-way street, liberating for employees, who gain clarity on what *great* looks like, and enlightening for leaders, who can themselves learn to be better servants.

I personally benefited from this sort of feedback when I sat down with my executive assistant Brandon to tell him I wasn't happy with his work. Too many of my priorities were falling by the wayside. Brandon, I should say, is a great guy – intelligent, a hard worker, and well able for the job he was hired to do. What I found through active listening was that Brandon was coming in early, staying late, and frustrated every day because he was being pulled in twenty different directions by powerful people within the organization, doing what he thought I wanted him to do. I realized that I had not shown Brandon his "6," what *great* looked like for his job, which should have been: to streamline my days and make me more effective.

Once Brandon and I exchanged feedback and discussed what *great* should look like for his position, his priorities shifted and his frustrations faded. He said later that he immediately felt focused and freed to do a good job. Not only did he begin completing all the work I needed done on a daily basis, it freed him to effectively use the Vision Traction Organizer (another helpful tool designed by Gino Wickman, author of *Traction*) to track quarterly and annual plans. You would not be reading this book today if he had not listed my becoming a published author in his plan.

A solid system for two-way feedback is the grease that allows the machinery of measurement to function, helping employees answer *yes* to the second of the Four Fundamentals of Employee Engagement, *Am I heard?* Having workers who know that they are listened to boosts motivation – and benefits the organization in innumerable ways. I can't imagine the strategic loss to our organization, for example, if the millennial salesperson who questioned our phone process hadn't spoken up because he thought no one would hear him.

The most important measurables, of course, the ones that we want all others to embody, as I mentioned early in this chapter, are our core values. Everyone at our organization knows that someone will be dismissed faster for a core values infraction at our organization than for any other issue. If you're careful about hiring, though, emphasizing your core values and the job's demands, carefully vetting all applicants, firing should be a rare occurrence. Most team members want to do good, and the deficits reflected in their metrics usually come back to management and communications issues.

Occasionally, you do wind up with someone who simply does not have the aptitude for a job or the desire to do it well. In that case, you could spend the rest of your life beating that dead horse – newsflash: it ain't getting up. My advice is to stick to the old adage, hire slow and fire fast. You're not doing the organization or the individual any favors by struggling to wedge a square peg into a round hole. Keeping someone around if he or she doesn't have the ability or desire to do a job actually violates our core value of "loves people." We want the best for all our team members and that means freeing the ones who don't fit here to find jobs elsewhere that they truly want and will be good at.

If team members have the desire and the aptitude for the job but don't really appreciate their role, the established systems, or the way you do business, it's up to you to get them on board. This, like so many challenges is part of effectively managing culture change, the subject of our next chapter.

THE TAKEAWAYS

- Most workers want to do great work, but leaders fail to convey what *great* looks like in terms that make sense for the individual team member's role and daily tasks.
- In creating metrics, leaders should focus less on the fruit (market share, sales volume, etc.) and more on the tasks and processes that produce it.
- Defining *great* intelligently, with process metrics, clarifies expectations, liberates employees, and helps them answer *yes* to the Four Fundamentals of Employee Engagement.
- In developing process metrics, leaders should:
  - Work backwards from the big goals to find the key fruit-bearing tasks you must measure to gauge performance for each individual.
  - Choose 3-5 vital measurables that will provide the best picture of performance and progress.
  - Realize everyone needs at least one if not several *daily* measures — waiting even a week to know how you're doing is too long.
  - Attach verifiable numbers to key metrics.
  - Explain to all team members the *why* behind their metrics to get buy-in and to show their importance in achieving larger goals.
- Good metrics depend on a strong two-way feedback system, which requires active listening and a fix-me-first attitude on the part of managers.

EXERCISE: TESTING YOUR METRICS

This simple exercise encourages leaders to try measuring employees in new ways, by the tasks and processes that create the end results, or *fruit*, as I like to say, rather than by the fruit itself. It can be tested on a small scale, with a single position, then expanded throughout an organization.

1. Write down all of your direct-reports and determine each of their roles in reaching your overall goals as an organization or department.
2. Within these individual roles, what are the 3 to 5 most important things that they do to ensure your success?
3. Determine reasonable expectations for each of these 3 to 5 critical tasks. This might require analyzing historical data or collecting new data to establish baselines.
4. These are your new metrics. For one month, measure your direct reports on these 3 to 5 things that produce results rather than on the results themselves.
5. Praise team members who are hitting their numbers and coach those who aren't, using active listening and two-way feedback to assess where problems lie.
6. How have your end results changed? How have the engagement and satisfaction levels of workers changed? How has your view of your direct reports' performance changed?

CHAPTER 6
Managing Culture Change

Culture change requires buy-in from all team members, detailed plans, accountability

When I found out why Jacob was really quitting, or as he put it, "why I'm not staying," he agreed to sit down with me to discuss his reasons and to explain where he thought the program was going wrong. He did not say that he would stay with the company, though, of course, I was hoping he would.

That meeting was a huge eye-opener for me. I've described Jacob's eight main objections to the way the program was being run. On a practical level, the biggest reason that Jacob gave notice was that the reality of the position did not match our job description. I have explained all the work that we did to attract college-educated career-minded millennials, creating a position that had a solid salary but didn't involve sales, commissions, or one-on-one negotiation. This was part of a broader cultural change at the organization, a new, more service-oriented approach to working with customers who, in the digital age, were doing their research online, before they called us.

As we saw in the previous chapter, however, the program was being undercut by middle managers who did not appreciate its *why*. They treated Jacob and the other Product Specialists as gofers half the time, fueling cars and running errands, and as pseudo-salespeople the rest of the time, with "sales" tracked on the board, though they weren't supposed to be selling.

Sitting down with me, Jacob explained that when his manager got busy, he expected the Product Specialists to negotiate with customers, too, something they were never supposed to do. This slippage, as well as tracking the number of sales resulting from their presentations, made Jacob and his peers feel as if they had been tricked into taking a sales job disguised behind a pretty title and empty promises.

Apart from our required online trainings, Jacob said that his manager gave these new employees little in the way of coaching or on-the-job training. In this environment, Jacob felt unwelcome and undervalued. Our mistake here was not taking the time to lay out what additional training would be required after the initial training period. Because we did not spell this out concretely, it fell to the wayside. This same mistake gets repeated in all sorts of businesses and in all industries. Truly changing culture requires setting specific goals and getting everyone on board.

Jacob didn't know where the message had gotten lost, of course, only that this was not the service-oriented job he'd signed on for. Since there was little training or coaching, he did not feel as if it would grow into that sort of position either, despite the path for advancement spelled out in our process manual.

These were the practical problems. On a deeper level, Jacob said, the organization and its leaders were not demonstrating their own core values. Misrepresenting the Product Specialist's role did not reflect the character and integrity we prided ourselves on, and this kind of leadership did not seem especially professional. Please understand that we have companies bring their management teams to our stores regularly to learn our strategies, and we always emphasize that the first step is ensuring that everyone fits our core values and is motivated by the same things. Turning these new hires into gofers, without the promised training or support, did not demonstrate our commitment to our core values. The servant attitude that underpinned the idea of a consumer advocate who did not sell or negotiate looked phony to Jacob, given his manager's behavior.

The objections that this young man raised during our meeting seemed right on the money. I promised him then and there that I was going to work to fix every one of them. I would do that whether or not Jacob stayed on, I said, but I wished he would consider sticking around to help me. I truly believed in this new kind of consumer advocate, a position that would work as advertised. In fact, I wanted it to be the cornerstone of a new business model for us and a paradigm for the industry, moving forward. It was no exaggeration to say that by staying with us, Jacob could be helping me and the organization and, in some measure, an entire industry with a cutting-edge program.

Jacob didn't answer right away, but when he called me the next day, he gave me an enthusiastic *yes.* Years later, he talked to my executive assistant Brandon about that decision.

"I put full trust in John," Jacob said. "So, the way my mind works, I'm never going to put 50 percent here and 50 percent there. I need to be 100 percent guaranteed bought-into one direction. I decided, hey, this is what I'm going to do. I want to put full effort into this. If I fall flat on my face, so be it, but I'm going to go full force with it."

From Jacob's perspective, my simply sitting down and listening (on the edge of my seat) to him created a lot of trust. My focus on listening (thank you, Amanda!) and fix-me-first attitude convinced Jacob that I was sincere and would try my level best to create the conditions in which he and the other Product Specialists could succeed.

"After that meeting, I knew that John was always going to have my back as long as I was doing the right thing," Jacob said. "I felt like, if my back was against the wall and others were against me but I was doing the ethical thing, by the book, he would be with me."

Jacob had never heard of the Four Fundamentals of Employee Engagement, but our meeting addressed them, resuscitating this talented but disengaged employee like a defibrillator jolting a stalled heart. He'd felt that he wasn't valued or heard, and that he wasn't growing. Now, the patriarch of the company had set up a meeting to hear him out and enlist his help in a mission-critical effort. By the time we finished talking, he most definitely felt that he was valued and heard and had an opportunity for growth.

ORGANIZATIONS ON AUTOPILOT

Effecting culture change is not easy, as I hope you appreciate by now. Picture the effort it takes to turn an oil tanker around. It's a slow process requiring a lot of energy, and there's an immense amount of momentum to overcome. Mistakes will be made, and course corrections will be necessary. This is why it's vital to have the fundamentals we've been exploring up to this point in place as you undertake a shift in organizational culture. Leaders are in a much better position to find and fix mistakes as they transform culture if they:

- Nurture the Four Fundamentals of Employee Engagement
- Practice active listening
- Employ two-way feedback with all employees
- Cultivate a fix-me-first attitude
- Demonstrate servant leadership

It was this style of leadership, which started with the lessons seven-year-old Amanda taught me, that spurred me to seek out Jacob when I heard he was quitting and insist on hearing his take. If I hadn't done that, I might have gone another six months or more before realizing our new program was veering off the rails. The fundamentals listed above also led me to the promise I made Jacob to fix what was wrong with the program and to deliver on our core values.

Of course, promises are easy. Making good on them can be tough, and I knew that we had a limited window in which to begin fixing the program and make real, lasting cultural changes. We had a new group of career-minded college-educated employees, and like Jacob, they were going to consider moving on if we couldn't make their job more like the one we'd advertised. If middle managers did not get fully on board with this program soon, it would only get harder to shift them from doing things the way they always had.

This sort of cultural transformation always reminds me of my boat, which has an autopilot feature. Occasionally, I grab the wheel to change directions, to avoid an obstacle or take a better route. I'll steer manually for a while and change our course temporarily, but as soon as I let my hand off the wheel, the boat reverts to the programmed coordinates – so smoothly it's hard to tell what's happening.

Organizations are like that boat. Grabbing the wheel to change directions is fine, but without setting a new destination and reprogramming the system, you will soon drift back to business as usual. This is human nature. Humans like the familiar, the tried and true methods they know, and who can blame them? *I know that doing X works. I've been doing it for twenty years. Switching to Y is risky and scary. What if it doesn't work?* So, after the first hiccup, people go back to what they know.

Fear and resistance are understandable, but you must overcome them in order to make progress. Wanting a transformation in culture isn't enough. Great ideas aren't enough. Enthusiasm isn't enough. This is where a written process, agreed by all, helps you stay the course, including dates and time frames for changes. You must also manage culture change, and in this chapter I'll explore some practical methods for doing so, the concrete tools that helped us deliver on my promise to Jacob and which I believe can help any organization transform smoothly and successfully.

Broadly speaking, these strategies can be divided into two categories – planning and people. Core values are at the heart of both, the rudder, as I noted earlier, that keeps your organizational boat on a true course once you've set the destination. You have to understand that if everyone does not embody and fit your core values, you will have forces pushing and pulling in different directions for various reasons, and the changes will never stick. The benefits of effectively managing culture change are enormous, both in terms of success and leaders' peace of mind. Failing to reprogram that autopilot, on the other hand, can drive leaders half insane as they keep racing back to the wheel and pulling hard to avoid obstacles, only to have the boat turn itself back toward the obstacle you were trying to avoid in the first place.

SYSTEMS BEAT GENIUS

We had created comprehensive manuals for Jacob's job, detailing every part of every process for his new position, but after I met with him, I realized that I had not taken the same care with the larger process of changing culture at our organization. Jacob's boss, for example, was supposed to be training and coaching these new employees and utilizing their talents in particular ways, but I hadn't given or asked for any specifics from him. Leadership had basically explained what should happen and then trusted that middle management would make it so.

A rollout like that was, first of all, foolish on my part. We weren't adding a new sales form or changing a step in our multi-point inspection. Product Specialists were new employees taking on an entirely new role which, as I've said, amounted to a new business model for us. It was not wise to think that the attendant culture change would simply happen, and it wasn't fair to expect managers to understand that this new position was crucial to our future simply because I said so.

Actions speak louder than words, but on paper (or screens) words can be given the weight of actions. When you are changing or creating processes as part of a cultural transformation, detailing individual tasks and procedures isn't enough. The implementation process also has to be put down in writing and agreed to by all, including middle managers. Smart leaders require written buy-in statements from managers, and documented plans for how they will develop new employees and implement changes. This may sound like a lot of work, but it really is as simple as presenting six or eight bullet points that managers commit to.

I have seen this phenomenon firsthand at our organization and throughout my career. Simply announcing a plan and getting verbal agreement gets you about 40 percent completion. The right written plan, with steps, a concrete timeframe, and built-in measurables will get you 70 to 80 percent to completion. As my old boss, Daryl, would say, "Systems are better than genius."

Daryl's old adage reflects the idea I've been promoting throughout this book that process-based organizations run more smoothly and effectively than talent-based ones. A smart, comprehensive plan in writing also conveys a level of seriousness that announced plans simply don't. I've explained that I did not really impress the *why* of our Product Specialist program on our managers, the people tasked with making it work on the ground. Well, getting them to put down in writing the various steps they'll take to make the program work is a great way to get managers contemplating the *why*.

And not all of middle management's inertia has to do with resistance to change or a love of the familiar. A new initiative like our Product Specialist program can seem overwhelming for managers who have only ever supervised salespeople paid on commission. Suddenly, they have new people filling a new role, trained, measured, and paid in new ways. A detailed written plan makes the transformation manageable – something that managers, understandably, like.

Organizations have their own preferences when it comes to planning, and everything I'm about to suggest can be customized to suit your needs. The basic principles of being thorough, however, with specific objectives, timeframes, and metrics hold true across the board.

A CLEAR PATH TO *GREAT*

When attempting to effect culture change, begin with an annual plan. What are the goals you hope to achieve one year from now? These can be as ambitious as you like, but they should be attainable if you want your plan to be taken seriously. With our new program, for instance, we might have started with the number of Product Specialists we wanted to have a year from inception, what levels we wanted them trained to, how many presentations we wanted them to have done, etc. (a caveat: when we started this program and set annual goals, the managers' tendency was to put down yearly expectations that were too high because they wanted to impress leadership – a common phenomenon). . These annual goals should be written out in as much detail as possible and circulated among leaders.

We're starting with the fruit here, but as we know from the previous chapter, **we want our team members focused on the things that produce the fruit. This is a critical point:**

- **Work backwards: break the annual plan down into quarterly goals and tasks that will get us to the end results.**
- **Ask what things will make the biggest difference in the next three months if we are to achieve our annual expectations.**

These fruit-bearing tasks don't all have to be financial. Some probably will be, but others might be behavioral or procedural. For instance, if our goal is creating a pleasanter environment, perhaps painting the front of our building or remodeling our bathrooms will get us closer to a goal. Maybe contacting a certain number of prospective clients in the next year, changing an inefficient process, updating a technology, or holding educational events will move us toward our targets.

Defining the fruit-bearing tasks that will get you to your goals should be a group effort. Middle managers are the ones on the ground who will oversee these tasks – or not, as we found out the hard way. Getting their buy-in by having them write detailed quarterly plans, laying out exactly how they'll move the organization toward the goalposts, is critical. We are not looking for elaborate written plans, but rather smart plans with four or five steps.

The quarterly goals should be broken down into weekly objectives that make the quarterly goals manageable, hold those completing tasks accountable, and keep everyone focused on the things producing the fruit. Moving backwards then, organizations should have three kinds of plans, each written out as intelligently as possible:

- Annual plan, broken down into...
- Quarterly plan, broken down into...
- Weekly objectives

How you handle those weekly objectives will determine your annual success. If they are vague or neglected, it's easy for an entire quarter to slip away with little or no progress. As always, these objectives should be in writing and as specific as possible. Good weekly objectives include the following:

- What you are hoping to accomplish
- Who will be accountable
- Who is needed to accomplish the task
- Dates of completion / timeframe
- How the objective will be measured

Let's look at an example. We announce that we want to increase training this year. Great, we've made a commitment. Typically, though, you get to the end of a busy quarter, and no additional training has occurred. With an annual plan that's broken down into quarterly plans and weekly objectives, it's much harder for this goal to slip through the cracks. If it does, you should know within a week that things are off track and have clarity on exactly who is responsible.

Looking at our annual training objectives, our trusted manager Bob might submit a written proposal to train a dozen of his team members in four different areas this quarter. Once senior leadership agrees that this is an appropriate goal, Bob writes out and submits the weekly objectives he'll tackle to get us there. His objectives list exactly what topics he'll be training on, who he is enlisting to help with that training, the dates that each piece of the training will be completed, and how each training will be measured. I am fully aware that as you read this, it might seem like a daunting task that will divert your employees' focus from production to work on the business. Please understand that the time you spend here, stopping the assembly line to fix these issues, will save you three times as much later, on the production end.

Bob's objective for week one might be to complete a written training schedule and send it to Carol and Chuck, whose assistance he needs, by March 15. Week two might involve reserving facility space for the trainings

(Chuck will do this by March 19), inventorying necessary training materials (Carol will do this by March 19), and ordering any necessary materials that we don't have on hand (Bob will do this by March 22).

Our first training, scheduled for the week of March 30, will be co-led by Bob and Carol – a one-hour session on best practices for welcoming customers. We will then measure trainees' knowledge on the topic with an online quiz they can take any time on April 3, and we'll measure the training's utility with an anonymous online survey following the quiz. The second training, scheduled for the week of April 14, will be a one-hour session on security led by…[see diagram below].

Hiester Automotive Group
2019 ANNUAL TRAINING PLAN
Quarter 1: January 1, 2019 to March 31, 2019

Annual Goals:	First Quarter Projects:	Weekly Objectives:
DUE: December 31, 2019	DUE: March 31, 2019	• Bob complete a written training schedule and send it to Carol and Chuck by March 15.
Goal 1: Increase employee training this year.	Quarterly Project 1: Bob submit a written proposal to train half a dozen of team members in four different areas.	• Chuck reserve facility space for trainings by March 19. • Carol inventory necessary training materials by March 19. • Bob order any necessary materials that are not on hand by March 19.
		• Bob and Carol co-lead a one hour session on best practices for welcoming customers by March 30.
		• Chuck build an online quiz to measure trainee's knowledge and quiz students by April 3.
		• Carol to lead training a one-hour training session on security by April 14.

Our Annual Training Plan; Broken down into
quarterly goals and weekly goals.

Quarterly goals are discussed in depth at our big quarterly meeting, and progress on weekly objectives at our weekly meetings. Those weekly meetings are critical, as are the metrics you're building into each objective. Before our organization began this sort of rigorous planning, we would ask at the weekly meeting, are you on track with that training or off track? Managers could easily claim to be on track but since the objectives weren't clearly specified, with completion dates and built-in metrics, we had no way of knowing for sure. In fact, to be fair, many managers probably answered such questions with a vague affirmative because they didn't really know what "off track" meant.

It's harder to claim you're on track when you've missed a completion date. With a quarterly plan and weekly objectives, we're showing mangers what *great* looks like and, just as we did with our process manual for Product Specialists, giving them a concrete path to get there. As we saw with metrics in the previous chapter, you can think of detailed plans as limiting or pinning managers down, but we believe that knowing exactly what is expected of you as a leader is liberating and frees you to be creative in other areas of your job.

Our organization tried several times, for example, to get our Customer Advocacy Program up and running in our Service Departments, and it fell by the wayside on each attempt. This wasn't just a source of frustration for me, but also for the managers tasked with making it work. It was only when we built this goal into our annual and quarterly plans, with concrete weekly objectives, that we finally launched it. The program was a success and became a point of pride instead of a source of stress for middle management. Your odds of success as an organization are about three times greater, in my experience, when you engage in the sort of planning I'm promoting here.

DARE TO DEMAND ACCOUNTABILITY

The comprehensive planning that allows you to effectively change processes, achieve goals, and transform culture is also a key part of delivering your core values. Remember that Jacob's first and perhaps biggest reason for not wanting to stay with us was that the company did not seem to be demonstrating its stated values. A lack of follow-through and accountability knocked us out of alignment with the principles we hold most dear and jeopardized a program important to our future.

Better planning, with quarterly goals and weekly objectives would have demonstrated to Jacob and the other Product Specialists that we have character and integrity – true servants who are professional and love people. Discussions of objectives in your weekly meetings as you work toward achieving quarterly goals is a chance to test decisions and strategies against your core values. Should we take approach A or B? Well, which one shows more of a get-it-done attitude? Approach B is cheaper, yes, but it does not demonstrate a love of people, while approach A does…

Changing culture requires reprogramming your organizational boat's autopilot, and as I suggested above, your core values act as a rudder. They help you to steer even a sizeable, complicated vessel and to maintain a true course.

The other way that we began thinking of our core values after my meeting with Jacob was as a promise. When we hired him and the other Product Specialists, we talked to them about our core values, as we always do in recruiting and hiring. A discussion like that is essentially a pledge to new employees that we are going to surround you with people who embody these core values. In Jacob's case, as he eloquently pointed out, we did not keep that promise.

After meeting with Jacob, I assembled all of our managers to make sure that they understood the *why* behind our Product Specialist program. Next, I met with our executive managers to assess our middle managers on core values by scoring them from one to ten in each category, understanding that a seven or below in any area would be cause to stop the assembly line. The direct manager that Jacob worked for got a low score in two of our five core values. My message to him was, "You have to fix this if you want to stay here. If you know you can't fix it, then it's easier to find a job while you have a job."

Let me stress that this manager was not incompetent or a bad guy in any way. In fact, he was and still is a friend. Our core values, as I noted earlier, are not for everyone. There are plenty of businesses in our industry where "loves people" is not on the list, for instance, much less in the top five. If you are "slow to hire" and emphasize your core values in recruiting, the vast majority of team members you bring on board will be on the same page. If, however, you have someone who does not share your core values and can't seem to develop them, you should be "fast to fire."

I'm saying "fire" here because that's part of the catch phrase, but "amicably part ways" is usually more accurate. Because we love our people and want the best for them as well as for the organization, we will tell them honestly: "You don't fit our core values and that deficit doesn't seem to be changing, so why not look for a job while you still have one?" This approach is so much better for all concerned than letting things get to a crisis point, or spending years trying to fit a square peg in a round hole.

By all means, give people a chance to get up to speed. There are many shortfalls that motivated workers with the right coaching and encouragement can overcome. We believe that everyone deserves fair warning and a solid chance. To be honest, however, a deficit in core values is often tough to get past. If "loves people" just isn't you, it's not a quality your likely to develop. We can all become better servants – I work on that every week – but if you don't already have somewhat of a "servant attitude," it's a tough hill to climb.

If you've adopted a "fix me first" attitude, communicated a clear plan, and explained the *why* behind tasks, and team members are still falling short, you have to consider what I call the DARE test:

- **D**esire. Do they have the Desire for it? Do they want to succeed in this position? Do they want to see the things they're tasked with achieving successfully completed?
- **A**bility. Do they have the Ability to do the job they were hired for and to complete the necessary tasks?
- **RE**cognize. Do they recognize, understand, and believe in it – the task in question, the organizational culture, the core values?

If people fail the DARE test, you can try until you're old and gray – they are not going to change course. In the case of Jacob's direct manager, our senior leadership team met to discuss his prospects. Everyone applied the

DARE test silently, on paper, so that no one would influence the others' assessments. We agreed almost unanimously that he **Desired** it but did not **Recognize** it, and most of us felt that he didn't have the **Ability** to do it.

If someone does not have the ability to do a job, the decision becomes easy. A position requires you to be on your feet all day and you have terrible knees? You're bad with numbers and work in accounts receivable? Those are looming disasters, unfair to both the employee and the organization. Likewise, someone who recognizes it but doesn't have the desire for it will probably do everything in his or her power, consciously or unconsciously, to derail it. Those who have the desire and ability but don't recognize it can sometimes be helped to see the light, but this was not happening with Jacob's direct supervisor.

We let him know the situation and parted on good terms. Keeping around people who fail the DARE test or who don't align with your core values will kill attempts to change culture. To return to my boat metaphor, they will at best revert to autopilot and, at worst, send you traveling in a circle, or even sink your vessel.

Let's review some of the steps we just explored for dealing with team members who appear to be blocking a change in culture:

- Make sure leadership agrees on perceived shortfalls
- Hold people accountable with written plans
- Listen actively to get a complete picture
- Emphasize the *why* behind incomplete tasks
- Assess the team member's core values
- Apply the DARE test
- Develop an improvement plan for those who fail DARE or part ways quickly, amicably

I should say that what happened with Jacob's manager is the exception, not the rule for us. As we assessed our staff, most of middle management did Desire it, have the Ability to do it, and REcognize and believe in it. In order to get follow-through, we only had to emphasize the *why* and help them with the sort of quarterly plans, weekly objectives, and built-in metrics we discussed above.

A process-oriented culture takes considerable work upfront, but over time, makes management immensely easier. One reason for that ease and one of the chief benefits of focusing on process is the longevity of team members. Surrounded by people with shared values utilizing efficient systems to achieve a common end, team members are more likely to stay with an organization for the long haul. Keeping employees long-term, however – especially career-minded college-educated millennials like Jacob – means that you must build careers not just jobs, the subject of our next chapter.

THE TAKEAWAYS

- Changing culture takes effort. Humans stick with tested methods, and organizations revert to what they know if they don't have detailed plans, metrics, and clear accountability.
- Core values serve as the rudder keeping your organization on a true course as you manage culture change.
- Smart leaders require written buy-in statements from managers and documented plans for how they will implement new processes. Simply having them commit in this way makes it three times more likely that they will complete the specified tasks without your involvement.
- Organizations should have:
  o Annual plan, broken down into...
  o Quarterly plans, broken down into...
  o Weekly objectives
- Weekly objectives make larger goals manageable, establish accountability, and keep everyone focused. Each objective should state:
  o What you'll do or change
  o Who is needed to accomplish the task
  o Dates of completion / timeframe
  o How the objective will be measured
- If team members are falling short, do a DARE test:
  o **D**esire. Do they have the Desire for it? Do they want to succeed in this position? Do they truly want to see tasks and goals successfully completed?
  o **A**bility. Do they have the Ability to do the job they were hired for and to complete the necessary tasks?
  o **RE**cognize. Do they recognize, understand, and believe in it – the task in question, the organizational culture, the core values?

EXERCISE: MAKE AN ANNUAL PLAN

Your ability to effect change and achieve goals improves dramatically when all parties not only commit to a transformation, but also deliver written plans with clear steps, timelines, and metrics for accomplishing various pieces of it. Use the template below to create an annual plan that's broken down into quarterly goals and weekly objectives.

Company Name
2019 ANNUAL PLAN

Quarter 1: _____ to _____

Annual Goals:	First Quarter Projects:	Weekly Objectives:
DUE: _____	DUE: _____	• Week 1: Due _____
Goal 1:	Quarterly Project 1:	

Template for Creating Your Own Annual Plan.

1. Begin with the goals you want to realize a year from now. Fill them in under the section labelled "Annual Goals."
2. Establish what you can do over the next quarter that will have the largest impact on achieving your annual goals. Fill these tasks in under the section labelled First Quarter Projects.
3. Discuss the annual and quarterly goals with your managers. Have them come up with written plans for achieving the portions of the quarterly goals they will be responsible for. Managers should break

those tasks down into "Weekly Objectives" and write them in that section. They must include the names of those who will help accomplish each task, target dates for completion, and individual metrics for each item.

4. This will allow you and managers to accurately confirm if things are "on-track" or "off-track."

CHAPTER 7

Build Careers, Not Jobs

Keep employees looking up, not out, with specific career ladders

I began this book with the news that my employee Jacob, exactly the kind of career-minded team member my organization wanted to keep, was quitting. I have explained why Jacob was important to the organization, how employees like him were part of a new business model and a change in culture for our company. I have detailed the philosophy behind creating positions and programs designed for a Jacob, as well as the obstacles it faced and the steps we took to remove them.

I have not, until now, told you what became of Jacob, whether or not the steps the organization took after I met with him were enough to engage him and similarly talented millennial employees. As you know well by now, I am a storyteller who enjoys narrative as much as a businessman who enjoys strategy, and what's a narrative without a little suspense?

The storyteller in me says that this is a good spot to tell you that Jacob not only stayed with the company, he rose steadily through the levels outlined in our Product Specialist handbook. As he progressed from Level 1 through Level 5, he gained valuable training and various certifications. His number of required product presentations rose alongside his training and experience, as did his pay.

Once Jacob passed Level 5 as a Product Specialist, he got certified as a notary and we sent him to Finance and Insurance Management School, as spelled out in the program manual. Completing this course doesn't guarantee a management job within our organization, but it prepares team members for the opportunity.

In Jacob's case, he was ready when a chance later opened up, and his Level 6 training allowed him to apply for a Finance Manager position within the organization. He began that job in a backup capacity and eventually became a full Finance Manager. Once he'd proved himself in that role and gained the requisite experience, he was eligible to apply for a job as a sales manager. As I write this, Jacob, who started with our company in an entry-level position not long out of school, is a successful sales manager with the organization, earning an attractive income as he oversees his own team of salespeople and Product Specialists who are starting where he did.

The kind of "ladder" that I'm outlining here – a major part of why Jacob stayed with the organization – used to be standard at American corporations, at least the best of them. When I first moved to North Carolina, IBM was the giant in this area. The company had set levels that employees could rise through and clear paths for growth. IBM team members understood that income rose with those levels, and they knew the requirements for each. They didn't just have *jobs*, they had *careers*. They had *futures,* and they rewarded the company while rewarding themselves by working their tails off, moving up the ladder, and sticking with IBM.

The retirement rate at IBM – the percentage of employees who built careers there right up to age sixty-five or older – was enormous compared to the rates at today's companies.

I want to encourage businesses to return to that older model of providing explicit paths forward for team members and building careers, not just jobs. Some companies already have seen the light here because they have no choice. After a long stretch of low unemployment, as I write this, a highly competitive labor market makes hiring and retaining talented employees extremely difficult, and organizations with clear career paths have a distinct edge.

Such organizations are more attractive to employees generally, but evidence suggests that they might be especially attractive to millennials, who are taking the reins of leadership and filling management positions. In a March 23, 2019 *Wall Street Journal* piece, Sam Walker, author of *The Captain Class: The Hidden Force that Creates the World's Greatest Teams*, quoted Gallup's employee engagement studies. He noted that beginning in 2002, survey respondents for the first time ever rated a rewarding job as their top priority, above family, having children, owning a home, and living in peace.

It's my belief that all humans want to feel like they're a part of something larger, that they're growing as individuals, accomplishing goals, and moving forward. For Jacob's generation, who grew up comparing lives on social media, this urge is perhaps especially strong.

In his *Journal* article, Walker cites Gallup's famous employee engagement stats, which document that roughly a third of U.S. employees are highly engaged on average, though at some top-notch businesses, the rate can rise to more than two-thirds. High levels of engagement have been linked to lower turnover, higher productivity, and greater profitability, and quality managers appear to play an outsized role in worker engagement. Given this dynamic, Walker suggests that strong middle managers might be the key to boosting not just employee motivation but the entire U.S. economy.

I agree with Walker, but here I want to emphasize that focusing on clear career tracks is a vital part of both cultivating strong middle managers and engaging employees at all levels. Realistically, it is not possible to achieve a high level of engagement with every single employee, but if every employee sees a path forward, your percentage of engaged team members will rise significantly. The best of those employees will climb the ladder you offer them and ultimately, become the high-quality middle managers that Walker argues are so important.

About now some readers are saying, that's fine for a giant corporation, but IBM we ain't. Let me assure you, neither is our business. I was once just as intimidated as you probably are right now at the prospect of thinking through career ladders for positions throughout the organization.

If you approach the process in the right way, though, it's not only doable, it makes management smoother and can boost productivity as well as your bottom line. This is true whether your business is IBM, a corner convenience shop, a general contractor, a bi-coastal ad agency, or a local clothes store. Team members can and should see a potential future within any business.

Not everyone wants to become CEO, true, but wouldn't it be great if everyone saw the pathway to get there?

STAY GREEN AND GROWING

I am a firm believer that you're either green and growing, or you're ripe and rotting. Whatever jobs we hold in our organizations, we all want to be around team members who are engaged, highly motivated, and inspired. Those who are "green and growing" tend to be more productive, energetic, creative, and just plain happy. The best way to have green and growing employees, I believe, is to spell out clear paths for advancement.

This thesis dovetails perfectly with the Four Fundamentals of Employee Engagement that I have returned to throughout this book. To review, they are:

- **Do I matter / bring value?**
- **Am I heard? Do I have a voice?**
- **Am I growing / developing?**
- **Am I fairly compensated?**

The third and fourth fundamentals directly address the kinds of career paths I'm encouraging. Team members who know with certainty that they have a future within an organization, one spelled out in concrete steps tied to training, experience, education, etc., appreciate that they work in a place where they can grow and develop.

If that path forward is also linked directly to income – the fourth Fundamental – team members are likely to feel that they are fairly compensated, too. Lots of employees want to earn more money. Those who know exactly what they need to do in order to get a specific pay bump are less likely to see their current pay rate as somehow unfair. *You think you should earn more? So do we – that's why we spelled out the following targets necessary for a raise. Your commitment was to complete Training X and achieve Performance Metric Y. What can we do to help you achieve these goals that you have fallen short on? Let's talk about these specifics and together, make a plan that can help you get to the next level…*

Having career-track discussions like this as part of quarterly conversations with employees goes a long way toward making them feel like they matter and that they are heard – the first two Fundamentals of Employee Engagement. Instead of the typical limited "review" in which team members are patted on the back and / or chastised, you're now having a deep two-way "conversation" about an individual's goals and future, and how they can be fulfilled within the organization. This is another term favored by Gino Wickman, author of *Traction,* who emphasizes such conversations as a space for exploring issues and setting priorities.

Compensation is important, but as I have said elsewhere, it is the least important of the Four Fundamentals. Yes, growth and performance should be tied to income, but too often, management focuses on pay while neglecting the individual's development and path forward. Compensation is the icing on the cake. Feeling that you matter, that you're heard, and that you are growing at your organization is far more important.

Those who believe that they are developing, with access to an obvious and specific "ladder" within the organization are less likely to look elsewhere. Without the detailed advancement path spelled out for our new Product Specialist position (more on that in moment), this job, like so many others, would have been a way for employees to bide their time while perusing the want ads until something better came along.

I saw this phenomenon firsthand when I started my own career. I worked for a company with a strong brand, excellent training, and fair compensation. There was a vague path forward – sales could lead to finance, which could lead to sales management, which could lead to general management – but it wasn't spelled out in writing and it wasn't specific to growth within that particular organization. Because management didn't focus on my future, I saw that I could advance along the same generic career path at any business in the industry, and maybe do it more quickly elsewhere.

This lack of focus on employees' career tracks within organizations is an endemic problem in American business today. I recently discussed it with my son-in-law, Bennett, in terms of his industry, banking, though you can find similar examples in almost any sector. As I discovered with my first job, Bennett said that in his experience, employees could move up in banking but that there was no clear path forward, with defined levels, training, performance requirements, and pay bumps. He explained far more eloquently than I could why this vagueness is discouraging for ambitious workers early in their careers:

"For someone coming out of college, yes, it's frustrating because we're programmed from kindergarten all the way through college to see the steps forward," Bennett said. "If you pass this class and do this, you go to second grade. If you do this, this, and this, you go to third, all the way up. In high school, if you get these SAT scores and these grades, you go to this kind of college. In college, your first and second year, you take your general education courses, then pick a major. If you get good grades, you get to pick the job you want in your field. We've been programmed that every ten months or so, you move into the next role. Then you get to a job where you might sit in the same role for years and years. Even though you're taking on new tasks and new projects, that doesn't necessarily mean you get a new job title or a new salary."

The result in banking, according to Bennett, is the same one I've noted in so many industries, including my own. The young talented employees who could be growing within the organization begin looking outside it for better opportunities.

"That's how they're trying to climb the ladder," Bennett said, "by bouncing from A to B to C, instead of staying at A and moving up to A2, A3, A4."

BUILDING CAREERS BUILDS CULTURE

Even team members who are generally happy with their daily tasks and compensation, who like their coworkers and bosses, who share core values and know they are part of some larger purpose, can feel that they are stagnating without a clear path forward.

Focusing on jobs rather than careers hurts retention, and any manager reading this understands that high turnover makes management more difficult. Consider the amount of time, energy, and money your organization devotes to hiring, training, and grooming new team members. Workers who stick around need less hand-holding, instruction, and supervision, and employees moving forward along a clear career path have greater loyalty to the organization long-term. On a daily basis, they are energized to prove themselves and solve problems. They look inward, not outward, with one eye always fixed on the next opportunity.

This kind of energy and productivity are vital to the kind of strong organizational culture I have explored in these pages. I would argue that no matter how powerful your core values and metrics are, no matter how well you are communicating and training, or how clearly you have defined *great*, it is difficult if not impossible to cultivate culture if you're suffering high turnover.

Boosting longevity obviously gives you a more experienced workforce. It also deepens institutional memory and adherence to core values. You want team members who get in their gut that *this* is how we do things at our organization. You want them thinking *our* organization, and this sense of ownership deepens with each year they are on board, advancing in their careers with you.

Jacob, who has risen from entry-level Product Specialist to sales manager, certainly exhibits that sense of ownership, as do many of those who started in the same program he did. A number of them have moved into leadership positions, becoming some of our most trusted and responsible managers.

As I write this, our business is in growth mode, purchasing additional stores, and to be honest, I'm not sure I would want to expand in this way if I did not have a deep bench within the organization. That bench was developed over years by establishing clear career tracks and advancing employees through the ranks. As I add two more stores, I will slot in two new finance managers who began their careers with us as Product Specialists, rose through the prescribed levels, and then attended Finance and Insurance Management school as spelled out in their handbook.

These two new finance managers aren't just qualified, with the right certifications and requisite experience – you can find lots of people with those credentials. It matters enormously that these team members rose through the ranks within our organization. They get and completely buy into our core values, our culture, and our way of doing things. My confidence in them, and in our organizational bench generally, is so high that an expansion that might have kept me up at night becomes fairly smooth, with minimal headaches.

In a very real sense then, workers who are green and growing fuel organizations that are green and growing. If yours isn't, it's time to consider establishing clearer career paths.

START AT THE END

I mean it when I say that you should attempt to delineate a path forward for every team member, including the dock worker, the delivery person, the gofer. Lots of terrific leaders start out in entry-level jobs, and you want to maximize your pool of talent, not send able people packing because they didn't see a way to advance.

I also understand that this might seem like an arduous task. Returning to the example of IBM, however, we can safely assume that the CEO did not sit down to personally draw every possible map leading from the mail room to a corner office. Neither did I. To build a bench and establish career paths, I only need to think about my direct reports. I make sure that they know how they can advance and that they are establishing concrete, written career tracks for their direct reports. Those managers must do the same for their direct reports, and so on, down the line.

This strategy doesn't just save work, it's more effective. The managers and supervisors throughout the organization truly understand what it takes to get to the next level because they're immersed in that part of the business. Frequently, they were in their team members' shoes not so long ago and worked their way up to the next level. The direct managers and supervisors should be the ones mapping these ladders, invested in their workers' futures and discussing them during quarterly conversations.

Let's look at a few fundamentals, using an example we're all familiar with by now, our organization's Product Specialist position. The strategy I'm about to present is not in any way particular to this job or to the automotive industry. The lessons apply to good leadership for any business in any industry. I'm using this position only as a convenient way to illustrate general principles.

In Chapter 5, "What does *Great* Look Like?" we discussed reverse-engineering good metrics, thinking about "the fruit," but then working backwards to focus on the things that produce the fruit. Building career paths works exactly the same way. What was our end goal with Product Specialists? We wanted to bring career-minded workers into the fold to offer our customers a high level of service and a new way of shopping in the Internet age, a model similar to that of the "Mac Geniuses" at Apple stores. We wanted these team members to stay with the organization, rising through the ranks as they gained experience and training until, ultimately, they could move into management.

Before building our ladder, we considered the negatives preventing these sorts of workers from joining and staying with the organization. I won't belabor this point, since we covered it in Chapter 1 and elsewhere, but we found that the main roadblocks keeping career-minded team members from building their careers with us were:

- **The stigma of being a car salesperson**
- **The uncertainty of commission-based pay**
- **Resistance to one-on-one negotiations**
- **Long hours**

We eliminated these career hurdles by creating a position, Product Specialist, that did not involve sales, commissions, or one-on-one negotiations (long hours had already been removed as an obstacle, so we simply had to communicate this reality). I encourage readers to engage in the same sort of analysis at their organizations, eliminating career barriers, before outlining paths for advancement.

This analysis also should be done with every position — and the strategy holds true for every business.

If you're a young engineering company that has trouble retaining engineers, frank discussions might reveal that while they were proud to graduate college and be hired at your firm, they're frustrated that moving past the entry-level tag is so difficult, and perhaps best achieved by moving to another firm where they will be viewed as having more seniority. For Product Specialists, it made sense for us to eliminate commission-based pay, but another company might have a position where making commission part of the mix for someone prospecting new business would lower attrition.

We want to grow our trees to get to the fruit, but before we start looking upward, we need to make sure that we address the impediments that will stunt growth and undercut our efforts. You might think of this basic step as making sure that the soil is fertile before seeds are even planted.

GIVE SPECIFICS IN WRITING

Once we are ready to look upward and build career ladders, they should include the following components, which I'll explore below:

- A written career path included in each position's handbook or manual
- Clear steps for advancement, with a label for each (a new title, level, designation, etc.)
- A clear career timeline that makes sense for the worker and organization
- Specific expectations for training, education, certifications, etc. tied to advancement
- Performance expectations for each step forward tied to numeric metrics
- Specific increases in pay and perks tied to steps forward

I want to note here that not everyone at your company will want to get to the next level. Some might be comfortable at Level 2. I am not insinuating that every person you bring into your organization wants to rise to Level 7, but establishing the potential path is critical. If someone does want to rise to Level 7, you'd better have a "ladder" in front of him or her. The ladder itself is often an incredible motivator, and some of those who seem as if they don't want to move up, you'll find, simply don't see a clear way to rise.

In Chapter 5, we discussed how metrics have to make sense for the organization and its economic model as well as for individual team members. The same is true for career paths, which should be closely intertwined with good metrics.

As I explained in Chapter 5, our organization calculated that the work of each beginning Product Specialist would have to result in around 6.5 sales per month in order to pay for the position and our bills, with something left over for profit. We absolutely did not want to measure these team members based on sales, but we knew from experience that four presentations resulted on average in one sale. Working backwards then, we could calculate that beginning Product Specialists would have to do around twenty-six presentations per month, or six per week, to hit our target.

During the first stage of their careers – Levels 1 and 2 in the chart below – Product Specialists would complete CRM (Customer Relationship Management) and NADA (National Association of Automobile Dealers) training, etc. The specifics of these trainings and certifications aren't relevant, but the degree of specificity is.

Whatever training and education benchmarks you decide make sense for a particular career ladder, spell them out as specifically as possible in writing: *earn Microsoft Office Specialist Excel Certification, complete CRM intro course, pass Professional Conduct and Regulation test,* etc. Avoid vague language such as "get comfortable with" or "gain experience on." Those are subjective standards that can be argued and interpreted. Passing a test or gaining a certification produces a paper trail everyone can agree on.

Similarly, new roles should have concrete new designations to recognize advancement and progress up the career ladder. For Product Specialists, as you've seen, we used a simple system, recognizing people as Level 1, Level 2, Level 3, etc. Another position might use common titles – junior associate, full associate, senior associate, etc. – or a code particular to your business.

The education, training, and experience required for each new title and each new rung on the career ladder should be tied to growing responsibility / performance goals, which can be measured by clear numbers, as well as increased compensation / perks. After 180 days, for instance, our Product Specialists can be at Level 3 if they have completed the trainings listed under Level 2 and are doing at least six product presentations per week. At that point, around six months in, they can begin earning almost 17 percent more than their starting salary and they are expected to do eight product presentations per week.

Product presentations are tracked on a 90-day rolling average that produces a hard number people are either hitting or they're not. Product Specialists should know when they head home each day where their average stands and exactly what they need to do to get to the next rung on the career ladder. If they aren't averaging eight product presentations per week at Level 3, they can't move up to Level 4, which comes with a 7 percent pay bump and more important, a feeling of accomplishment and forward momentum. If all goes well, the team member thinks, *yes, my level of responsibility is increasing, my hard work is being recognized, and I'm just one level away from qualifying for Finance and Insurance Management School, which will give me a shot at a management position.*

You'll note from our example that the rungs on this career ladder are structured in quarterly, or 90-day, increments. These track nicely with our quarterly conversations and make sense for this position. You might have careers where the first rungs are defined every two months, or four or six months. Find a timeline that makes sense for the organization and for team members. Be careful, however, not to rush someone up the ladder. Moving people up too quickly, before they're ready or comfortable, can actually be discouraging – the opposite of what we want. Likewise, waiting too long to move someone up, though the next rung is spelled-out clearly, can kill engagement and spur workers to start browsing the want ads.

The career ladder I've printed here as an example is part of our Product Specialist manual. As you know from our discussion of Written Repeatable Process in Chapter 4, I am a big fan of establishing processes and committing them to paper and servers. Your team members should have easy access to this sort of framework, showing them exactly where they are, what they must do to climb the next rung, and the added duties and pay they'll receive once they get there.

Product Specialist
CAREER LADDER

Level 1: $$/ week
> Trainee for 90 days. Takes BDC appointments only

Level 2: $$/ week
> Eligible after 90 days.
> - Fully certified in manufacture training
> - CRM training complete
> - NADA training complete
> - Eligible to enroll in GM Mark of Excellence or Chrysler Academy Rewards
> - Minimum of 6 product presentations per week

Level 3: $$/ week
> Eligible after 180 days
> - Minimum of 10 product presentations per week, 90 day rolling average

Level 4: $$/ week
> Eligible after 240 days
> - CSSI for Chevrolet has to be above national average on question 10 and 14
> - CSI for Chrysler has to be above local sales advocacy
> - Minimum of 14 product presentations per week, 90 day rolling average

Level 5: $$/ week
> Eligible after 300 days
> - Must attend Notary class
> - Take NADA class for F&I
> - CSI has to be maintained per manufacturer guidelines
> - Minimum of 18 product presentations per week, 90 day rolling average

Level 6: $$/ week
> Eligible after 1 year of employment
> - Enrolls in F&I school
> - CSI must be maintained per manufactured guidelines

Level 7: $$/ week
> Eligible after 18 months of employment
> - F&I school complete
> - Begin manager training in GM Global Connect and NADA
> - May interview for different jobs in the store: Sales, F&I, Manager

---

By signing below, I acknowledge that I have reviewed and understand the Product Specialist Career Ladder.

Employee Signature	Date	Manager Signature	Date

Product Specialist Career Ladder. Remember, you want to increase your salary amounts as you progress up to each new level.

HELP EVERYONE TO GROW

Jacob, as I noted, became an excellent Finance Manager and then a top-notch sales manager after working his way up as a Product Specialist. Another talented team member named McKenzie started in the same program, but somewhere around Level 4, decided that she did not want to follow the remainder of that career ladder or attend Finance and Insurance Management School.

McKenzie is a hard worker who excelled in the program and shared our core values, but sometimes team members don't realize they're on the wrong path until they reach a certain height on the ladder. In McKenzie's case, we started looking at other opportunities within our organization that would better fit her life, goals, and interests. Ultimately, she elected to go into our service drive, becoming part of our initial Customer Advocate Program, a lane that she now manages.

McKenzie's story illustrates another benefit of considering careers and the future throughout the organization rather than focusing only on workers' immediate jobs. An exceptional person who fit our culture was able, with our help, to find another track that was more satisfying to her personally, and eventually, to thrive in it. This is good for her and good for the organization – it keeps both "green and growing." Concrete career tracks encourage team members who might otherwise linger in a position that they don't love to focus on and take control of their futures. For the organization, it's about maximizing talent and engagement levels.

I would be lying if I didn't acknowledge that building career ladders is a work in progress for our organization. Many positions, from sales staff to auto technician, have clear paths for advancement. For others, we have not yet fleshed out clear career ladders – a fact highlighted lately when a receptionist greeting applicants for a job in our accounting office asked me, "What would I have to do to be considered for that position?"

Our receptionist needs a path forward, too, and she didn't have one, or at least, not one with the sort of clear opportunities our Product Specialists have.

Most executive managers start in an entry level position at some point in their careers. That receptionist may very well be your CEO one day. On the other hand, occasionally, someone does not fit any of your career tracks or, it becomes clear, belong at the organization. If you're slow to hire and you're emphasizing your core values in recruiting, this should be a rare occurrence. When it does happen, clear career ladders highlight those who aren't moving forward, the weak links who can't seem to get beyond Level 2, or whatever your earliest designations are.

If someone isn't suitable for the job he or she was hired for, or for another within the organization, you should be "fast to fire" just as you should be slow to hire. "Amicably part ways," as I've noted, is perhaps a better way to phrase this separation, since we really do believe that it's in the best interest of the individual as well as of the organization to move on.

Keep the talented employees who belong in their positions green and growing with career tracks. Release those who will linger ripe and rotting if they stay at your organization, so that they can thrive somewhere else.

THE TAKEAWAYS

- Historically, successful American companies such as IBM established career tracks to keep team members engaged and growing long-term within the organization.
- Low unemployment and a competitive labor market make retaining talented employees difficult, and organizations with clear career paths have a distinct edge.
- Focusing on specific, clear career ladders is a vital part of both cultivating leadership – building a strong "bench" in-house – and engaging employees at all levels.
- You're either "green and growing" or "ripe and rotting." Career ladders keep workers green and growing – productive, energetic, creative, and happy.
- Work backwards from your end goals for engagement and leadership to develop career ladders for your direct reports. Have them do the same for their direct reports, etc. down the line.
- Career ladders should include:
  - A written guide to advancement in each position's handbook or manual
  - Clear steps for advances, with labels for each
  - A clear career timeline that makes sense for the worker and the organization
  - Specific expectations for training, education, etc. tied to advancement
  - Performance expectations for each step forward, tied to numeric metrics
  - Specific increases in pay and perks tied to steps forward
- Clear career ladders highlight those who aren't engaged. Part ways with these workers quickly for everyone's benefit.

EXERCISE: BUILD A CAREER LADDER

1. **Pick a position**, or job, to begin. To build a career ladder for it, start at the end, with "the fruit." What sorts of employees do you want in this position? If they excel, what sort of leadership roles or enhanced responsibilities would you like to groom them for? (In our Product Specialist example, we wanted college-educated career-minded team members who could work their way up to leadership positions such as Finance Manager and Sales Manager.)

2. **Identify impediments.** Before you think about the specifics of advancement, or rungs on the career ladder, ask what obstacles might keep this job from attracting or retaining your ideal candidates. Do your best to eliminate these impediments. (In our Product Specialist example, we identified and eliminated these obstacles: the salesperson stigma, commission-based pay, one-on-one negotiations, and long hours.)

3. **Set performance requirements.** You know your expenses. Working backwards from them, calculate how much entry-level employees earning reasonable pay in this position must produce in order to justify their checks, pay the bills, and leave something for profit. This performance minimum should be a concrete number easily accessible to the employee (in our Product Specialist example, we determined that the work of these new hires must result in 6.5 sales per month for the job to be economically viable. Since we knew that 4 presentations resulted in 1 sale, starting Product Specialists would have to do 26 presentations per month, or 6 per week).

4. **Decide on training, education, experience.** What skills, education, and training do you want workers in this position to acquire in order to advance? Be specific, focusing on concrete tests, certifications, classes, etc. Decide on a logical order and a reasonable timeline for achieving these milestones (in our Product Specialist example, we listed key milestones, ranging from full manufacturer training certification to NADA training).

5. **Establish concrete advances, or rungs.** Thinking about the previous two steps, outline a series of concrete career advancements tied to increased training, performance, and income on a detailed timeline. After, say, 90 days on the job (or 4 months or 6 – whatever makes sense for you), when several key training milestones have been reached, what would be a reasonable increase in performance requirements? What would be a fair, corresponding pay increase? Consider the same questions of training, performance, timing, and income for the next logical step up the career ladder. Each step should be named concretely, with a designation that is recognized throughout the organization. Tailor the number of steps or levels to the position in a way that makes sense for the organization – could be 3 or 10, depending (the sample career ladder we printed in this chapter for our Product Specialist position demonstrates how progress in training, performance, and income can work together to keep employees engaged when spelled out on a concrete timeline).

6. **Include in manual / handbook.** To be effective, your career ladders should be written down and printed in each position's manual, where employees can easily access it (our Product Specialists are given a manual that includes the career ladder we printed in this chapter on their first day).

7. **Review career progress.** During regular conversations, have managers discuss team members' career progress with them, offering praise for advancement and pointers for tough patches (we focus heavily on career ladders during our quarterly conversations, but because our performance requirements for positions like Product Specialist are measured daily, we are continually addressing employees' growth).

CHAPTER **8**

Troubleshooting and Course Correction

Building better processes to address challenges never stops

When our business was small, we had one of the best Customer Satisfaction Indexes for the industry, not just in our state but all of the Southeast. In fact, we once took possession of a traveling trophy for having the top CSI for the entire year. As our business grew, however, maintaining a high Customer Satisfaction Index became more difficult. We rode a rollercoaster. The CSI was high when we focused on it, but as we got busy and things slipped, so did our ratings.

Of course, when our CSI sagged, we noted more complaints, voice mails, and customer concerns. We examined the problem and saw that most of our complaints came from people whose cars had been with us more than five days awaiting repairs. Once again, I'm telling a story from the car business because it's what I know best, but my friends in fields ranging from construction to accounting assure me that it's the same in their businesses. When customers have a problem, they want it addressed quickly and they want to know how long it will take. Delays and inaccurate information are the enemies of customer satisfaction in every industry.

It was my executive assistant, Brandon, who during one of our weekly meetings, brought up the issue of too many Repair Orders (ROs) taking too long. How bad was the problem? We analyzed the data and saw that at one large store with a high volume of business, we had eighty or ninety ROs that were more than five days old. A medium-sized store had sixty or seventy, and our smallest store had forty to fifty Repair Orders open longer than five days.

A lot of dealerships wouldn't blink at these numbers. Many factors affect repairs, including delays in getting needed parts from the manufacturers – something that seemed largely beyond our control – but stepping back to assess the situation from our customers' perspective, we knew that such excuses wouldn't matter. Having this many ROs open more than five days was simply unacceptable.

We came together as a leadership group to focus on this problem, using a *Traction* strategy called IDS – Identify, Discuss, Solve. The basic idea is that rather than lingering, issues go on a list, get prioritized, discussed, and solved. Applying this method, we arrived at the solution that our General Managers would have to address all aging ROs during morning meetings with their service managers. The situation improved for a while and then, of course, started to slide once more. We talked to the managers again, and complaints diminished. A few weeks later, the number of open ROs once again creeped up.

My frustration level was off the charts, and I was tempted to make the rounds for a healthy dose of yelling. That, no doubt, would have fixed the problem temporarily yet again – and no doubt, the numbers would have begun sliding again within a month. Instead, in the spirit of "fix me first," I thought about the situation and realized that it was my fault. This issue, like so many in business, was a problem of process, and we had tried to solve it with a mere verbal remedy, writing nothing down.

Starting over, we decided what *great* looked like (our end goal, or "the fruit," as I like to say), designed an effective process with clear steps to get there, wrote that process down, and made one person accountable for following it.

What did *great* look like here? At the large store that had eighty to ninety ROs open for more than five days, we said that we did not want more than twenty-five on average open that long. The middle store should not average more than twenty, and the smallest store fifteen.

To achieve *great* at each store, we devised concrete steps and a clear process for General Managers to follow. The General Manager should:

1. Identify why the vehicle is here more than five days.
2. Verify that reason, not just internally but externally, too. If we're waiting on a part, call the manufacturer to confirm and discuss the delay.
3. Look for an alternative way to get the part. If our contact at the manufacturer confirms the delay, talk to his or her boss to discuss the holdup. Find out if there is there any way around it. Is the part available locally, at another store?
4. Communicate where things stand to the customer, with our apologies.
5. Revisit the issue, looking for an alternative every single day that the RO remains open.

We agreed that our General Managers would be fully responsible for this process and that we would be tracking the number of Repair Orders open more than five days on a three-month running average. It was another example of a principle I discussed early in this book: *If everyone is accountable, no one is accountable.* With our first attempts to tackle the problem, accountability was spread around, and excuses were rife. Now, if we got a complaint, our General Managers understood that we were not going to the service writer or to the mechanic, we would go straight to them to ask, *Why is this RO open more than five days? Did you contact the manufacturer? Did you look for alternate parts locally?*

The General Managers knew that they'd better have answers to these questions – and they knew that handling this well would be rewarded.

By making aging Repair Orders a priority, determining what *great* looked like, and establishing a written process to get there, we achieved unbelievably good results. Within one month, all of our stores had fewer than twenty-five Repair Orders open more than five days, and around 95 percent of our complaint calls disappeared.

CONTINUAL COURSE CORRECTION

The process I just outlined is what I mean by "troubleshooting," or "course correction," in the title of this chapter. Very simply, this is the ongoing process of identifying the areas within your business that aren't meeting your expectations. I say "ongoing" because this is a never-ending effort.

No matter how strong your core values are, how intelligent your metrics, how open your communication, or how effective your strategies, problems will arise. Efforts will fall short. Some customers will be dissatisfied, and there will always be a better way to do something. This is where troubleshooting and course correction come in.

In some ways, the Repair Order story that I opened this chapter with is a confession. I run multiple successful businesses. I have been at it for decades. I have read widely on business methods and learned, often through painful trial and error, strategies that I think are extremely effective. My leadership team and I have transformed culture at our organization, with strong core values, innovative sales strategies, world-class training, solid metrics, and all of the other tools we've explored in these pages.

I have enough confidence in these techniques that I literally decided to write the book on them and yet, I not only let our open Repair Orders rise to an uncomfortable level, I initially tried to address what was clearly a process problem with mere conversation. I should have known in my bones that this issue cried out for Written Repeatable Process.

Such mistakes happen in every business in every industry during the chaos of the workweek, and they always will. As long as people are involved in business, troubleshooting will always be necessary, and to be honest, it's part of the fun, or it should be. You probably wouldn't be reading this book or work in business at all if, on some level, you didn't believe this.

I did not enjoy seeing our Consumer Satisfaction Index bob up and down or hearing that our aging Repair Orders had gone off the rails. I did not enjoy chastising managers when the problem did not get fixed the first time we addressed it. I did, however, enjoy rolling up my sleeves and deciding with my senior leadership team what *great* should look like for our Repair Orders. I enjoyed sweating through the steps of a Written Repeatable Process that would ultimately cut our complaint calls by more than 90 percent and make us much better servants, demonstrating our professionalism and love of people.

One of the biggest sources of frustration in business is the repeated application of Band-Aids to the same cuts. True course correction heals the wound. It is more time-consuming and difficult, but designing an intelligent process in response to challenges and problems rather than a quick, temporary fix saves massive amounts of time and frustration in the long-run.

This, as I've said, is true for every business whether you sell ice cream, houses, or software, whether you offer consulting, legal, or dog-walking services. Every business has its version of our Repair Order problem, an issue with customer satisfaction, poor scheduling, slow response times, or perpetually messy display shelves.

Whatever the flashpoints are in your business, I would urge you to step back and forget about what the industry says. Forget about "normal." Forget the accepted practices and standards. Look at your business from a fresh angle and ask yourself, what am I unhappy with? How would I like it to look?

Troubleshooting often makes me think of the television series, *The Profit*. If you haven't seen this reality show, it stars Marcus Lemonis, a self-made millionaire and charismatic entrepreneur who turns struggling businesses around.

Lemonis goes in and evaluates the situation and the business, considering the kind of organization it should be, the sorts of products it should carry, the changes it will need in order to succeed. Then he simply puts together a plan and builds processes that will allow the business to achieve those end goals. He interviews the parties involved, assessing their roles and where their heads and hearts are. He doesn't use our term, "core values," but operates on the same principle – those who don't fit the plan have to go.

The biggest difference between this approach and the Band-Aid approach is the investment of time upfront. Analyzing the situation carefully takes time and effort, but done well, it saves you the pain and frustration of addressing the same issues over and over. Often, with some fairly minor and inexpensive adjustments (remember my aging Repair Order example, which cost almost nothing beyond a little extra time and care), you can right the ship, get back to making money and pleasing customers and fulfilling your original vision.

DECIDE WHAT GREAT LOOKS LIKE

The first step in effective troubleshooting might look complicated. You have to step back, consider the problem or challenge with fresh eyes, and decide what *great* looks like. What is the end goal, the ultimate vision? Where do you want your sales numbers, production volume, customer reviews, delivery times, etc. in three months or six, or in two years?

This can be complicated because even the best managers are creatures of habit. Correcting course might mean changing the way something has been done for decades or the way that everyone else in the industry does it. You're likely to meet resistance internally or externally, or from both directions at once. In my earlier example, delays in getting parts from manufacturers at first looked like an insurmountable wall. *Sorry, waiting on a part, nothing we can do about that, right? Just the way it is, way it's always been.*

But where there is a vision and a concrete standard for *great*, there is a way. Eighty to ninety Repair Orders open beyond five days is not acceptable. I would like to eliminate *all* Repair Orders that old, but after examining the data, we determined that lowering that average to no more than twenty-five would be doable.

Determining what *great* looks like is as much an art as a science, which is why it's important to collect and analyze as much relevant data as you can. For example, we have software that monitors every Repair Order, so it's easy to isolate and track those that have been open more than five days. Looking at the historical data and trends, we could see that there were times when we had far fewer than eighty aging Repair Orders at our largest store. Analyzing this info helped us arrive at targets that were ambitious but realistic.

We score every piece of our business in similar ways. We know how many vehicles we want to sell and how many people we have to talk to in order to get there. If we don't realize the requisite number of presentations, then we know that we have an advertising problem or an inventory problem. If our closing percentage is off, we know we have a sales process problem. If appointments shown are off, we know we have a Business Development Center problem.

Again, the specifics of my business here aren't important. The point is that if you have a bad week or a bad month and you're flying blind, you won't know where to go to fix the problem, or later, how well your fix is working. If you're not already collecting the relevant data, troubleshooting might require doing a little research on your own business, tracking numbers and processes in new ways to make the best possible choices.

There is an element of investigation here. You have to be willing to "stop the assembly line," to borrow William Deming's phrase, and listen to all involved parties while analyzing data to determine the underlying causes of whatever problem or shortfall you're experiencing. Addressing our Repair Order problem involved talking not just to our General Managers, but also to our Service Managers, Parts Department, mechanics, manufacturers, and others to get a complete picture.

DESIGN A PROCESS

I would start by making a list of nine or ten things that you wish were different, better, or more efficient. Start with the one that you think will have the largest impact. Decide what great would look like if that process, person or situation were improved. Once you have decided what *great* looks like, design a process that will allow you to achieve it. Your process should address any roadblocks in the way of your goals and provide specific steps and tools for those tasked with getting you there.

In my troubleshooting example of aging Repair Orders, we were essentially asking our General Managers to troubleshoot smaller problems in the same way that we were troubleshooting the larger one. First, they would have to identify the problem, as we had. We labelled the overall problem "aging Repair Orders" and gathered as much data as we could about it.

Looking at his or her oldest Repair Order first thing in the morning, one of our General Managers might name this problem "missing part." After identifying the problem, the General Manager would have to verify it both internally (with the service manager) and externally (with the manufacturer), gathering as much info as possible about the delay in getting this particular part.

Already the process battle is half won, and we haven't even taken any remedial action. Why do I say this? Because with those first two steps, we engaged a manager to name a problem and gather necessary information about it. This might seem trivial, but as everyone on my staff knows, I firmly believe that until you name a problem, you have no chance of solving it.

By identifying the problem and gathering info about it, our General Manager is now paying attention to it, and that is the most important piece of this process. We knew from tracking our own data that our averages on aging Repair Orders slid when we stopped paying close attention to them, and so, our process had to codify care, to guarantee that attention would be paid.

The next part of devising a course-correcting process is critical: provide concrete steps for a solution. In our example, the general manager has identified and named the problem, verified it both in-house and with the manufacturer. Step 3 in the list above, then, is to talk to the boss of our contact at the manufacturer. We want to make sure our contact has it right and isn't missing an alternative way to get the part faster. Sometimes this quick phone call can solve the problem. If it doesn't, the next standard step is to look for the part locally. Often, we can send a driver over to another store and have the part within the hour rather than waiting days, but if no one bothers to check, the delay groans on.

These steps are simple, specific, and verifiable. We're no longer asking did you "try" to get the part? The inevitable answer to that question is, yeah, I "tried." But what exactly does "try" mean? Everyone's definition is different. Now, the questions are: *Did you call Dave Smith, our contact at the manufacturer? Did you call Sue Taylor, his supervisor to double check? Did you call the local stores to see if the part is available here?* The General Manager knows exactly what to do and has a specific yes-or-no checklist.

The final two steps in our process are to inform the customer of where things stand, and then to revisit the issue the next morning if the RO remains open. In my example, customers are directly affected as they await their vehicles, but even if you're troubleshooting a problem that's primarily internal, with only a distant or indirect effect on customers, it's vital to keep them in mind as you design a process correcting course. They are the reason you're in business. Everything affects your customers in some way, and every process, ultimately, is about them. The greatest thing about addressing problems with written process in this way is that it's preventative. Building our process largely prevented Repair Orders more than five days old because middle managers now knew that the senior leaders were watching, and they corrected the problems before they ever got to five days.

WRITING, ACCOUNTABILITY KEY

Of course, a process is only as good as the paper (and computer) it's written on.

The written word has weight. There's a reason that not a day passes without analysts and politicians framing proposals and laws and issues in terms of the U.S. Constitution. It is our guide and touchstone. It's the law of the land and must be followed. Changing it is difficult, and straying from it has serious consequences.

You want whatever process you design while troubleshooting to carry the same sort of authority as an amendment to the Constitution, which is why you have to write it down. You can tell managers what you want as clearly and as loudly as you want, but until it's written down, you won't get follow-through. This was the mistake I made initially with our Repair Orders, simply *telling* our managers to address the problem.

If they weren't written on stone tablets, the Ten Commandments would have been interpreted as the Ten Suggestions and probably forgotten long ago. We don't need to carve every process in stone, but paper or a digital file that becomes part of a manual is the modern equivalent.

Similarly, we built in clear metrics – a rolling average of no more than 25 open Repair Orders at our biggest store, for example – which were indisputable and could be reviewed daily. Strong metrics also boost accountability, putting everyone on the same page and establishing firm goal posts.

Some processes are necessarily complex, with lots of steps, but don't make them even a smidgen more complicated than they need to be. Use clear, direct language and strive for simplicity. This leaves less space for interpretation and it increases accountability. One person, as I've said, should be held accountable for seeing a process through – in our case, this was the General Manager. Yes, others, ranging from service managers to workers in our Parts Department, are involved in various steps, but the buck stops with the General Manager. That is the person we're holding fully accountable, the one I'm coming to question if Repair Orders veer off the rails.

As I've said elsewhere in this book, I don't see accountability as punitive in the least. In my model of leadership, accountability is freeing. People generally want to do good, and accountability is the tool that helps them do it. By the time we'd finished troubleshooting our problem with aging Repair Orders, our General Managers had a clear roadmap for how to reduce open ROs and dramatically boost customer satisfaction. They were as happy as I was to see our customer complaints cut by 95 percent within a month. They enjoyed the bonuses attached to their targets obviously, but the pride and satisfaction of doing a good job and being better servants was far more important.

THE TAKEAWAYS

- Troubleshooting, or course correction, is the ongoing process of identifying the areas within your business that aren't meeting your expectations and addressing them.
- True course correction requires a process. It aims for a long-term solution, not a quick fix.
- Strong leaders try to see a problem with fresh eyes when troubleshooting. They ignore the accepted, the usual, the industry standard. They find their own unique "6."
- Gather as much data as possible in order to design a better process. This might mean doing some research on your own business.
- Always write the improved process down when correcting course and hold one person accountable. Remember, *if everyone's accountable, no one is.*
- Accountability is freeing. People want to do good, and accountability is the tool that allows them to.

EXERCISE: MAKE A COURSE CORRECTION

The quick fix takes a day, sometimes just hours or minutes, but it usually offers temporary relief at best. True course correction involves deeper analysis. It means taking a step back, stopping the assembly line, and assessing a challenge with fresh eyes. Gathering data, deciding what *great* looks like, and designing a new or improved process is hard work, but investing that time and energy upfront saves it on the back end. Effective troubleshooting not only makes management easier, it helps your managers become better troubleshooters in their own right, improving the organization's service across the board. Below is a broad outline of the steps we use in troubleshooting and course correction.

1. Identify and name the problem or challenge you're facing – whether it's a production bottleneck, inefficient scheduling, supply-chain issues, weak marketing, etc.
2. Gather all relevant data and information regarding the problem. Discuss the challenge with all relevant parties. This might include multiple managers, workers, and departments within your operation, as well as manufacturers, vendors, service providers or others outside it.
3. Decide what *great* looks like in terms of this challenge. What's the vision or end goal? Be careful to look at the problem with fresh eyes. Forget about what's accepted, how things have been done, and industry standards. Find *your* "6," as Charles M. Schwab did at Andrew Carnegie's steel mill.
4. Design a process solution with concrete steps that will get you to your vision and which can be verified. Make the steps as few and as simple as possible.
5. Write the process down as clearly as you can and make it accessible.
6. Hold one person accountable for seeing the process through. Others might be involved in achieving goals, but let one person know that it's his or her job to see that goals are reached. This

is who will be questioned about how well the steps of your new process were followed if it fails – and rewarded if it succeeds.

7. Build verifiable metrics into the process for monitoring and follow-up. If adjustments prove necessary, you want to make them based on data, not pure trial and error.

CONCLUSION

Why Your Jacob is a Vital Asset

This book, as you know by now, isn't really about Jacob the person, despite its title. Rather it's about the idea of Jacob, or a Jacob. For our organization, Jacob is a stand-in for the kind of career-minded employee we determined we needed in order to thrive and grow. More broadly, he represents the human resources that form the core of your business, whatever your ideal employee profile is.

Finding, developing, and engaging *your* Jacob over the long-haul is critical, no matter what industry you work in, no matter what your organization produces or provides. Recruiting *your* Jacob starts with deciding on *your* core values, which will be – must be – different from mine and your competitors'. Your core values represent the unique character and personality of your organization, the things you hold most dear. They are what separate you from the pack and ultimately, provide you with competitive advantage, the rudder guiding the organizational ship.

Prioritizing those core values when you advertise, interview, and train will draw team members who share them – your Jacobs – into your organization. Once they are on board, engaging and retaining these team members depends on working at the many strategies we have discussed here. Developing world-class training, good metrics, Written Repeatable Process, career ladders, and the other elements we've explored is key.

These strategies build on the Four Fundamentals of Employee Engagement. Simply keeping these four questions in mind as you develop programs, processes, and policies will build trust and go a long way toward engaging team members. No manager or organization is perfect, but if employees feel that they matter, that they are heard, growing, and fairly compensated, even significant missteps can be corrected with minimal damage.

Key to everything we've discussed here is what I have called "servant-leadership." This style of leading, which grew from the lessons a seven-year-old named Amanda taught me, puts a premium on active listening and always seeks to "fix me first."

If your core values are strong and you're using them to recruit, if you are slow to hire, then you will get your Jacob, the right person for the job, most of the time. Once you know that employees were right for the job when you hired them and that people generally want to do good, you can view most problems as issues of *process*. What is the manager, the team, the organization doing that's preventing employees from doing good? Where is the breakdown in accountability, metrics, management, Written Repeatable Process?

If followed, all of these practical steps and strategies add up to a deep change in culture. The result is an organization with less of an us-them mindset, less yelling, finger-pointing, and firing. Those poisonous dynamics are replaced with increased accountability, more data, more analysis, and intelligent processes, which because they are written down and repeatable, consistently create better experiences for both team members and the customers they're serving.

It all begins with leaders creating that initial vision and deciding what *great* looks like. Once you determine what you want, the path to achieving it will appear, just as it did for me once I wrote "water pressure" on a yellow legal pad and for Charles Schwab once he chalked that "6" on the steel mill floor. Such a simple principle and yet, in the fog and frenetic pace of the busy workday, even experienced leaders – and I include myself here – can ignore it, applying Band-Aids, putting up with chronic problems, letting good enough be good enough when they could have *great*.

It all boils down to the simple sentence I have repeated throughout this book and will leave you with now, the one thing I hope every reader takes from these pages:

You get what you settle for if you don't know what you want.